Milk
Sugar

GRANDMA'S
FAVORITE
DESSERTS

ISBN 13: 978-1-58581-009-3
ISBN 10: 1-58581-009-6

Printed in the United States of America

Interior Book Design: The Printed Page, Phoenix, AZ

Golden West Publishers
4113 N. Longview
Phoenix, AZ 85014
(800) 658-5830
(602) 265-4392

For free sample recipes for every Golden West cookbook, visit **www.goldenwestpublishers.com**. Also see our additional site at **www.cookbooksusa.com**.

Contents

Kitchen - Family

Don't those words just GO together? A passel of our fondest family memories are eternally linked to the heady aroma of grandma's apple pie, a plate load of spaghetti, or her super-savory pot roast. Some of our beloved cooks may no longer be in the kitchen, but a momentary wave of sadness is replaced with an urgent need to pull out our favorite grandma recipe, along with some smiling memories. I began jotting down my vivid recollections of Grandma's kitchen...evoking a bounty of beautiful recollections. Before I knew it, I was asking everyone I met to tell me about their grandma-in-the-kitchen stories...and the best are here to entertain you while your dish chills, bakes, or simmers...

An image of an apple pie cooling on the windowsill still makes us smile when we think about dessert time with Grandma. It might seem outdated, but it's an image or even a feeling that we all wish we could have again. Memories of a simpler time.

What is the best way to conjure up those old feelings or recreate them for our kids? Well, the best way would be to make those old-fashioned recipes the old-fashioned way. Like Grandma used to make them. We might have a few shortcuts these days, but we don't have to sacrifice quality with modern convenience. In fact some modern methods can make grandma's desserts even more delicious than they originally were.

So sit back and let's go back to that simpler time when cookie dough wasn't found next to the butter in the grocery store and cakes didn't come from the freezer section. Let's bake the way Grandma used to and savor the taste of yesteryear…today.

LinDee's Grandma Irma aimed for perfection in her kitchen, right down to peeling potatoes. She taught LinDee the nuances of potato peeling – with a paring knife, not the flimsy peeler that sent brown strips flying with a flick of the wrist. Less elbow grease, less time and if you did it right, more potato was her motto. LinDee's cousin and his parents visited from the city one day and Ron challenged her to a "potato peel-off." He, using the trendy peeler and she using Grandma's trusty paring knife. They squared off at the big, porcelain sink with two potatoes each. "Ready… set…" her Grandma chuckled and paused another long second, "go!" They were off. Valiantly, LinDee sliced thin and fast, but was no match for her smug, fancy-peeler cousin. "That's okay," Grandma Irma said with a smile, "Winner gets to clean up the mess."

CAKES

Cakes

Sarah loves antiques. She became interested in collecting when her Grandma Thelma bequeathed a kitchen full of vintage appliances and serving dishes, along with *her* Grandma Winifred's china and baking utensils. Sarah soon found that decorating her kitchen with the quaint pieces made great nostalgic and conversational accents. Her favorite was the small Bromwell's "Bee" flour sifter. A friend, always looking at old things with an eye for renovation, told Sarah the old, dull silver-colored sifter could use a makeover. After a little bright green paint, a dainty floral decal and a new perch on the windowsill, Sarah thought she heard Grandma's lighthearted chuckle, and smiled at the transformed sifter luxuriating in its retirement.

Amazin' Raisin Cake

3 cups **Flour**
2 cups **Sugar**
1 cup **Mayonnaise**
1/3 cup **Milk**
2 **Eggs**
2 tsp. **Baking Soda**
1/2 tsp. **Ground Cinnamon**
1/2 tsp. **Nutmeg**
1/2 tsp. **Salt**
1/4 tsp. **Ground Cloves**
3 cups peeled and chopped **Apples**
1 cup **Seedless Raisins**
1/2 cup chopped **Walnuts**
2 cups **Whipped Cream**

Preheat oven to 350 degrees.

Grease and flour two cake pans. In large bowl with mixer at low speed, beat the first ten ingredients 2 minutes. Stir in apples, raisins and nuts. Pour into pans, and bake in preheated oven for 45 minutes or until done. Cool in pans for 10 minutes. Remove from pan and let cool. Frost with whipped cream.

Banana Split Cake

1 cup melted **Butter**, divided
2 cups crushed **Graham Crackers**
2 cups **Powdered Sugar**
1 tsp. **Vanilla**
2 **Eggs**
3 or 4 **Bananas**
1/2 can (4 oz.) **Crushed Pineapple**
1 container (16 oz.) **Cool Whip® Whipped Topping**
1 cup chopped **Nuts**, optional
1/4 cup **Maraschino Cherries**, optional

Mix 1/2 cup of butter with the graham crackers and press into a 9 x 13 inch pan. Melt the other cup of butter and mix with sugar, vanilla and egg. Beat on high for 5 minutes. Pour the sugar mixture over the graham cracker crust. Cut the bananas in half lengthwise and dip the bananas into the crushed pineapple. Lay the bananas side by side on the sugar mixture and spoon the crushed pineapple over the bananas.

Spread with the Cool Whip® and chill for 4 hours. Garnish with nuts and cherries.

Blueberry-Orange Coffee Cake

2 tbsp. **Butter**
1/4 cup **Boiling Water**
1 tbsp. + 1 tsp. grated **Orange Peel**
1/2 cup + 2 tbsp. **Orange Juice**
1 **Egg**
3/4 cup **Sugar**
2 cups **All-Purpose Flour**
1 tsp. **Baking Powder**
1/2 tsp. **Salt**
1/4 tsp. **Baking Soda**
1 cup **Fresh Blueberries**
2 tbsp. **Honey**

Preheat oven to 350 degrees.

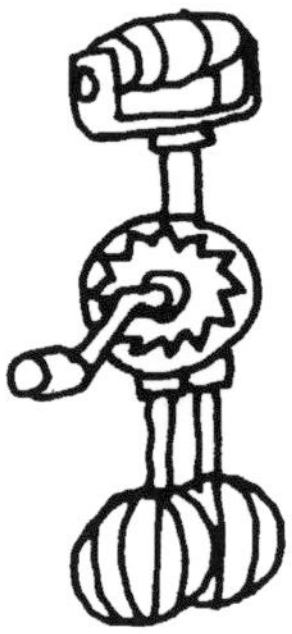

Combine butter and boiling water in a small bowl. Add 1 tbsp. grated orange peel and 1/2 cup orange juice. Set aside.

In a large bowl, beat egg and sugar together with an electric mixer until light and fluffy. Set aside.

In a medium bowl, combine flour, baking powder, salt, and soda. Add flour mixture to egg mixture, alternately with orange juice mixture. Beat well after each addition. Fold in blueberries. Spoon into a lightly greased pan of your choice. Bake in preheated oven for 55 minutes. Remove from oven, and cool in pan for 10 minutes.

Glaze: Combine 1 tsp. grated orange peel, 2 tbsp. orange juice, and 2 tbsp. honey, mixing well. Put a wire rack over a paper towel. Remove coffee cake from pan to the wire rack. Spoon orange/honey glaze over coffee cake. Let cool before slicing.

Carrot Cake

1 cup **Vegetable Oil**
1/2 tsp. **Baking Soda**
2 1/2 tbsp. **Boiling Water**
1 1/2 cups **Sugar**
3 **Eggs**, separated
1 1/2 cups **Cake Flour**
1 tsp. **Baking Powder**
1/2 tsp. **Salt**
1/2 tsp. **Cinnamon**
1/2 tsp. **Nutmeg**
1 cup grated **Carrots**
1 cups chopped **Nuts**
1/2 tsp. **Vanilla**
1 cup **Raisins**, optional

Preheat oven to 350 degrees.

Grease and flour a 10 x 14 inch pan. Thoroughly mix all the above ingredients except egg whites. Beat egg whites until stiff. Fold into flour mixture. Bake in preheated oven for 35 minutes. Cool and frost.

Frosting:

2 1/2 to 3 cups **Powdered Sugar**
2 tbsp. grated **Orange Rind**
3 tbsp. melted **Butter**
Juice of 1 small **Lemon**
1 or 2 drops **Orange Food Coloring**, optional

Mix all of the above ingredients together until smooth. Make sure that the frosting is a little thick. If needed add more powdered sugar.

*Non-stick bakeware will typically make a darker crust and glass tends to cook more quickly. You'll have to make some adjustments based on your own preference.

Champagne Cake

1 box (18 oz.) **White Cake Mix**
1 package (3 oz.) **Instant Vanilla Pudding**
8 oz. **Cream Cheese**, softened
1 1/2 cups **Milk**
1 can (8 oz.) **Crushed Pineapple**
16 oz. **Cool Whip® Whipped Topping**

Prepare cake mix as directed on the box, and bake in a 13 x 9 x 2 inch pan until done. When cake is completely cooled, mix instant pudding, softened cream cheese and milk until smooth. Spread on cake. Drain the pineapple and spread over pudding mixture. Frost with Cool Whip® and refrigerate until ready to serve.

Optional fruit toppings: Cherry or **Blueberry** pie filling may be used. When in season use fresh crushed **Strawberries.**

Chocolate Chip Cake

1 bar (8 oz.) **Chocolate Baking Bar**
1 box **Yellow Cake Mix**
1 box (3 oz.) **Instant Vanilla Pudding**
1 cup **Vegetable Oil**
4 **Eggs**
1 cup **Milk**, reserve 4 tbsp.
6 oz. **Chocolate Chips**
1 1/4 cup **Powdered Sugar**, reserve 1/4 cup

Preheat oven to 350 degrees.

Grate the bar of chocolate. Set aside 1/4 cup of the grated chocolate to use later.

Mix cake mix, vanilla pudding, oil, eggs, milk, remainder of grated chocolate, and then stir in the chocolate chips. Bake in a greased bundt cake pan in preheated oven for 50 minutes or until done. While baking, mix one cup of sugar and 4 tablespoons of milk together. Once the cake is done, turn it out of the pan immediately.

Glaze the hot cake with the powdered sugar and milk mixture. When the cake is just about cooled sprinkle the 1/4 cup of grated chocolate and 1/4 cup of powdered sugar over the cake.

Chocolate Sheet Cake

1 cup **Water**
4 tbsp. **Cocoa**
1 cup **Butter**
2 cups **Flour**
2 cups **Sugar**
1/2 tsp. **Salt**
1 tsp. sifted **Baking Soda**
2 **Eggs**
1 cup **Sour Cream**

Preheat oven to 375°.

Grease and flour a medium size cookie sheet, 13 x 9 x 2. In a pot mix the water and cocoa together until heated. Add the butter and bring to a boil. Remove from heat; add flour, sugar, salt, and soda. Beat in eggs and sour cream until smooth. Pour into pan and bake in preheated oven for 22 minutes. In the same pan you used to mix the other ingredients (without washing pan) mix frosting while cake is baking.

Frosting:

7 tbsp. **Milk**
1/2 cup **Butter**
4 tbsp. **Cocoa**
1 lb. **Powdered Sugar**, sifted
1 cup chopped **Nuts**

Mix milk, butter and cocoa in pan over low heat until butter melts and the mixture is smooth.

Add powdered sugar and mix ingredients. Pour in nuts and mix well. Frost when cake is warm.

*When making a chocolate cake, try using cocoa powder instead of flour after greasing the pan.

Easy Carrot Cake

3/4 cup **Butter Flavored Shortening**
1 cup **Sugar**
2 **Eggs**
1 tsp. **Vanilla extract**
4 1/2 oz. **Heinz® Instant Baby Food, Carrot Flakes**
2 tsp. **Cinnamon**
2/3 cup **Water**
1 cup **Flour**

Preheat oven to 325 degrees.

Cream shortening and sugar. Add eggs and vanilla extract, beat well. Add carrot flakes, cinnamon and water. Mix well, gradually adding the flour. Place in a greased loaf pan and bake in preheated oven for 45 minutes.

Frosting:

1 package (4 oz.) **Cream Cheese,** softened
1 tsp. **Vanilla Extract**
1/4 cup **Butter Flavored Shortening**
8 oz. **Powdered Sugar**

Mix cream cheese, vanilla, and shortening until smooth. Add powdered sugar and beat well, until fluffy and light. Frost cake.

Fantastic Chocolate Cake

2 cups **Sugar**
1 cup **Butter**
1 tbsp. **Vanilla**
2 oz. **Dark Chocolate**, melted
4 **Eggs**
1 tsp. **Mayonnaise**
1 tsp. **Salt**
2 tsp. **Baking Powder**
1 tsp. **Baking Soda**
1/2 cup **Cocoa Powder**
1 box (3 oz.) **Instant Chocolate Pudding**
1 cup **Milk**
2 cups **Flour**

Preheat oven to 350 degrees. Grease and flour bundt pan or two cake pans. Mix sugar, butter, vanilla, chocolate, eggs and mayonnaise until creamy. Add salt, baking powder, soda, cocoa, and chocolate pudding and beat on low until mixture is blended together. Add milk, and gradually add the flour. Bake in preheated oven about 30–40 minutes.

Judy's Fudge Cake

3 oz. **Unsweetened Chocolate**
1/2 cup **Butter**
2 1/4 cups lightly packed **Brown Sugar**
3 **Eggs**
1 1/2 tsp. **Vanilla**
2 tsp. **Baking Soda**
1/2 tsp. **Salt**
2 1/4 cups **Flour**
1 cup **Sour Cream**
1 cup **Boiling Water**

Preheat oven to 350 degrees.

Grease two cake pans. Melt chocolate, set aside. In large mixing bowl, cream butter until smooth. Add brown sugar and eggs. Beat with mixer on high speed until light and fluffy, about 5 minutes. With mixer on low speed, beat in the vanilla, melted chocolate, soda and salt. Add flour alternately with sour cream, beating on low until smooth. Pour in boiling water, stir with spoon until blended. Then pour into cake pans. Bake in preheated oven 35 minutes or until done.

Cool in pans. Turn on wire racks to cool completely. Frost if desired.

Old-Fashioned Shortcake

Shortcake:

2 cups **Flour**
1/4 cup **Sugar**
3 tsp. **Baking Powder**
1/2 tsp. **Salt**
1/2 cup **Butter**
3/4 cup **Milk***

Strawberry Topping:

3 pints fresh **Strawberries**
3/4 cup **Sugar**
1 cup **Heavy Cream**
2 tbsp. **Powdered Sugar**

Preheat oven to 400 degrees.

Lightly grease 8 x 8 x 2 inch square baking dish. Sift flour, sugar, baking powder, and salt into large bowl. With pastry blender or 2 knives, cut in butter until mixture resembles coarse cornmeal. Make a well in center of mixture. Pour in milk all at once; mix quickly with fork, just to moisten flour. (Do not over mix). Turn dough into prepared pan. With fingers (dipped in a little flour), lightly press dough evenly into bottom of pan.

Bake in preheated oven 15 minutes, or until golden.

Meanwhile, make topping; wash strawberries in cold water; drain. Reserve several nice strawberries for garnish. Hull and slice remaining berries. Add sugar; mix well. With beater, beat cream just until stiff. Gently stir in powdered sugar.

To Serve: Loosen edges of cake with knife, and turn out on serving plate. Put bottom on serving plate, cut-side up. Spoon half of sliced berries over layer. Set top of cake in place, cut-side down. Spoon remainder of sliced berries over the top. Mound whipped cream lightly in center. Garnish with whole strawberries. Serve at once. Makes 9 servings.

*To get better texture in your cake use **Buttermilk** when the recipe calls for milk, adding 1/2 tbsp. of **Baking Soda** per 1 cup buttermilk to cut the acidic value. You can create your own buttermilk by adding either 1 tbsp. lemon juice or vinegar to 1 cup regular milk.

Orange Cake Deluxe

1 cup **Butter**
1 cup **Sugar**
3 **Egg Yolks**
1 cup **Sour Cream**
Grated rind of 1 **Orange**
1 3/4 cups **All-Purpose Flour**
1 tsp. **Baking Powder**
1 tsp. **Baking Soda**
3 **Egg Whites,** beaten to peaks

Preheat oven to 325 degrees.

Cream butter and sugar. Add egg yolks, sour cream and orange rind; beat until light and fluffy. Sift together flour, baking powder and baking soda. Stir into first mixture. Fold in egg whites, which have been beaten until stiff but not dry. Turn into oiled and floured bundt mold. Bake in preheated oven for 1 hour. Remove from oven and let stand for 10 minutes. Loosen carefully around edge and turn out on platter with a rim. Pour hot orange syrup over top of cake slowly. Reserve some to serve with cake.

Orange Syrup

Juice of 2 **Oranges**
Juice of 1 **Lemon**
3/4 cup **Sugar**
Dash of **Salt**

Combine ingredients. Boil 3 to 4 minutes.

Orange Crunch Cake

Crunch Layer:

1 cup **Graham Cracker Crumbs**
1/2 cup firmly packed **Brown Sugar**
1/2 cup chopped **Walnuts**
1/2 cup melted **Butter**

In small bowl, combine the ingredients together until crumbly. Press half of crunch mixture into each prepared pan.

Cake:

1 package **Yellow Cake Mix**
1/2 cup **Water**
1/2 cup **Orange Juice**
1/3 cup **Oil**
3 **Eggs**
2 tbsp. grated **Orange Peel**

Preheat oven to 350 degrees.

In large bowl, blend cake ingredients at low speed until moistened; beat 2 minutes at highest speed. Pour batter evenly over crunch layer. Bake in preheated oven for 30 to 35 minutes or until done. Cool 10 minutes; remove from pans. Cool completely.

Frosting:

1 can **Pillsbury® Vanilla Frosting Supreme**
1 cup **Frozen Whipped Topping**, thawed
3 tbsp. grated **Orange Peel**
1 tsp. grated **Lemon Peel**
1 can (11 oz.) **Mandarin Oranges**, drained or **Orange Slices**
Mint Leaves, optional

In small bowl, beat frosting until fluffy; add whipped topping and continue beating until light and fluffy. Fold in grated orange and lemon peel. Place one layer, crunch side up, on serving plate; spread with 1/4 of frosting. Top with remaining layer, crunch side up. Spread top and sides with remaining frosting. Arrange orange sections on top. Garnish with mint leaves. Store in refrigerator.

Peach Cobbler

1 1/2 cups **Sugar**, reserve 1/2 cup
1 cup **Flour**
1 tsp. **Baking Powder**
1/4 tsp. **Salt**
6 tbsp. melted **Margarine**
1/2 cup **Milk**
1 can (8 oz.) **Sliced Peaches**

Preheat oven to 375 degrees.

Mix together 1 cup sugar, flour, baking powder and salt. In another bowl, stir 3 tablespoons margarine and milk until creamy. Mix together. Butter a 9 x 13 pan and pour in batter. Add the sliced peaches. Sprinkle 1/2 cup sugar on top and remaining 3 tablespoons margarine. Bake in preheated oven for 40 to 60 minutes.

Shortcut Coconut Cake

1 box **Yellow Cake Mix**
2 cups **Sour Cream**
2 cups **Sugar**
2 packages **Frozen Coconut** or
3 cans **Angel Flake Coconut**

Preheat oven to 350 degrees.

Bake cake in 9-inch cake pans, as directed on cake mix box. Split layers. Stir together sour cream, sugar and coconut. Use as filling between layers and on top of cake. Wrap or cover cake and let stand in refrigerator 2 days. Keep refrigerated.

Pumpkin Roll With Frosting

3 **Eggs**
1 cup **Sugar**
2/3 cup canned **Pumpkin**
3/4 cup **Flour**
1 tsp. **Baking Powder**
2 tsp. **Cinnamon**
1 tsp. **Ginger**
1/2 tsp. **Salt**
1 cup finely chopped **Pecans**
1/2 cup **Powdered Sugar**

Preheat oven to 375 degrees.

In one bowl beat the eggs for five minutes on high speed. Gradually beat in the sugar and then stir in the pumpkin. In another bowl add the flour, baking powder, and spices, blending well. Next fold the pumpkin mixture into the flour mixture. After mixing, pour into a well-greased 15 x 10 x 1 inch pan and sprinkle with the chopped pecans, covering completely. Bake in preheated oven for 15 minutes. Turn out onto a cotton towel, and then sprinkle with powdered sugar. While still warm, carefully roll the short end, along with the towel and let cool. Begin frosting while the roll is cooling.

Frosting:

8 oz. **Cream Cheese**
4 tbsp. **Margarine**
1 cup **Powdered Sugar**
1/2 tsp. **Vanilla**

Soften the cream cheese and margarine. Gradually add the powdered sugar. Once the frosting becomes creamy, add the vanilla. Unroll the pumpkin roll and remove the towel. Frost and roll up again. Chill and serve sliced or whole.

Streusel-layered Coffee Cake

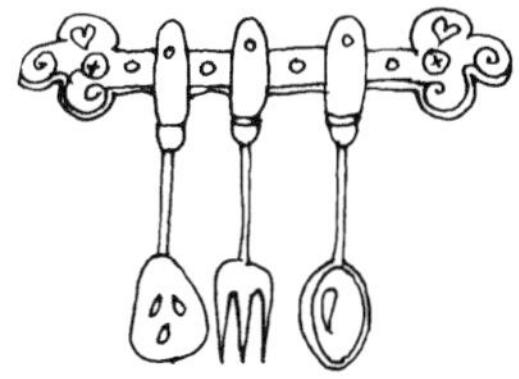

Streusel:

1/2 cup **Brown Sugar**
2 tbsp. softened **Butter**
2 tbsp. **All-Purpose Flour**
1 tsp. **Cinnamon**
1/2 cup chopped **Walnuts**

In a small bowl combine brown sugar, soft butter, flour, cinnamon and nuts; mix with fork until crumbly. Set aside.

Batter:

1 1/2 cups sifted **Flour**
2 1/2 tsp. **Baking Powder**
1/2 tsp. **Salt**
1 **Egg**
3/4 cup **Sugar**
1/3 cup melted **Butter**
1/2 cup **Milk**
1 tsp. **Vanilla**

Preheat oven to 375 degrees. Grease 8 x 8 x 2 baking pan.

Sift flour with baking powder and salt. Set aside.

In medium bowl, beat egg until frothy. Beat in sugar and butter until well combined. Add milk and vanilla. With wooden spoon, stir in flour mixture until well combined. Turn half of batter into prepared pan.

Sprinkle evenly with half of streusel mixture. Repeat with remaining batter and streusel mixture. Bake in preheated oven 25 to 30 minutes. Cool slightly on wire rack. Serve warm.

Makes 9 servings.

Sunday Special Coffee Cake

Topping:

1/2 cup **Sugar**
1/4 cup sifted **Flour**
1/4 cup softened **Butter**
1 tsp. **Cinnamon**

Preheat oven to 375 degrees.

Grease an 8 x 8 x 2 inch baking dish. In small bowl, combine sugar, flour, butter and cinnamon. Mix lightly with fork until crumbly. Set aside.

Batter:

1 1/2 cups sifted **Flour**
2 1/2 tsp. **Baking Powder**
1/2 tsp. **Salt**
1 **Egg**
3/4 cup **Sugar**
1/3 cup melted **Butter**
1/2 cup **Milk**
1 tsp. **Vanilla**

Sift flour with baking powder and salt. Set aside. In a medium bowl, beat egg until frothy then beat in sugar and melted butter until well combined. Add milk and vanilla. With wooden spoon, beat in flour mixture until well combined. Pour into prepared pan. Sprinkle topping evenly over batter. Bake in preheated oven 25-30 minutes. Cool partially, in pan. Cut into squares while still warm.

Makes 9 servings.

Swedish Apple Cake

1 1/2 cups **Sugar**
2 **Eggs**
1/2 cup **Shortening**
1 tsp. **Vanilla**
1 1/2 cups **Flour**
1 tsp. **Cinnamon**
1 tsp. **Soda**
1 tsp. **Nutmeg**
Dash of **Cloves**
3 cups **Apples**, diced with skins on
1/2 cup chopped **Nuts**
3 tbsp. melted **Butter**
3 tbsp. **Milk**
1 1/2 cups **Brown Sugar**
Whipped Cream
Maraschino Cherries

Preheat oven to 350 degrees.

Grease and flour a 13 x 9 x 2 inch pan. Cream sugar, eggs, shortening, and vanilla together. Sift flour, cinnamon, soda, nutmeg and cloves together. Add to cream mixture. Add apples and nuts. Stir until mixed. Pour into pan and bake in preheated oven for 25 minutes. Mix butter, milk, and brown sugar together until smooth. Spread this on top of cake after it has baked for the first 25 minutes and bake again for an additional 25 minutes. Serve with whipped cream and maraschino cherries if desired.

Yam Cake

2 1/2 cups sifted **Self-Rising Flour**
1 tsp. **Cinnamon**
1 tsp. **Nutmeg**
1 1/2 cups **Vegetable Oil**
2 cups **Sugar**
4 **Eggs**
1/4 cup **Hot Water**
1 1/2 cups finely grated raw **Sweet Potato**
1 tsp. **Vanilla**
1/2 cup **Raisins** (optional)
1 cup chopped **Pecans** or **Walnuts**

Frosting:

1 can (14 oz.) **Evaporated Milk**
1 cup **Sugar**
1 stick **Margarine**
3 **Egg Yolks**
1 tsp. **Vanilla Extract**
1 1/2 cups **Flaked Coconut**

Preheat oven to 350 degrees.

Grease and flour three 8-inch round layer cake pans. Sift flour and spices together in a mixing bowl, and set aside. In a large mixing bowl, combine cooking oil and sugar. Beat in eggs one at a time. Add hot water. Fold in flour-spice mixture. Stir in sweet potatoes, nuts, vanilla, and raisins. Combine thoroughly. Turn batter into pans and bake in preheated oven 30 minutes or until done.

Combine all frosting ingredients EXCEPT vanilla and coconut in a saucepan. Cook over medium heat, stirring constantly, until thickened (about 20 minutes). Remove from heat. Add vanilla extract and coconut and stir. Let cool. Spread frosting between layers and on top of cake.

Zucchini Cake

3 **Eggs**
2 cups **Sugar**
1 cup **Vegetable Oil**
1 tsp. **Salt**
1 tsp. **Baking Powder**
1 tsp. **Baking Soda**
1 tsp. **Vanilla**
1 tsp. **Cinnamon**
1/2 tsp. **Nutmeg**
1/8 tsp. **Allspice**
2 cups shredded **Zucchini**
1/4 cup **Milk**
3 cups **Flour**
1 cup chopped **Walnuts**

Preheat oven to 350 degrees.

Grease and flour bundt pan. Mix together eggs, sugar, oil, salt, baking powder, baking soda, vanilla, nutmeg, allspice and cinnamon. Beat on low speed for one minute. Add zucchini and milk and blend together. Gradually add the flour and beat at medium speed until smooth. Stir in the walnuts and pour into pan. Bake in preheated oven for 1 hour and 10 minutes. Cool in pan for 15 minutes, then on wire rack until completely cool.

Chocolate Cake

"This cake was a family favorite on my grandmother's farm."

Elaine Hansen, Union Grove

4 squares **Chocolate**
1 cup **Water**
2 cups **Sugar**
1/2 cup **Shortening**
4 **Eggs**
2 tsp. **Baking Soda**
1/2 cup **Sour Cream**
2 cups **Flour**

Preheat oven to 350 degrees. In a double boiler, melt the chocolate and combine with water. Cream together the sugar and shortening, add chocolate mixture, then mix in the eggs one at a time. Combine baking soda and sour cream and blend into sugar mixture, alternating with flour. Pour batter into baking pans and bake in preheated oven for 40 minutes.

Küchen

"This recipe was given to me by my German grandmother."

Mary C. Beau, Green Bay

Crust:

1 tsp. **Sugar**
1 cake **Yeast**
1/4 cup **Warm Water**
2 tbsp. **Sugar**
1/2 tbsp. **Salt**
1/4 cup **Shortening**
1/4 cup **Boiled Milk**, cooled
1 **Egg**
2 cups **Flour**

Add 1 teaspoon sugar and yeast to warm water and let sit until yeast dissolves. Cream 2 tablespoons sugar, salt and shortening together; add yeast mixture and stir in milk, egg and flour. Cover and let rise until double in size. Pat dough out into bottom and sides of an 11x15 cake pan.

Filling:

2 cups sliced **Apples**
3/4 cup **Sugar**
1/4 cup **Butter**
1/2 tsp. **Cinnamon**

Layer apples over crust. Cream sugar, butter and cinnamon together and dot over surface of apples.

Topping:

1 cup **Sugar**
3/4 cup **Flour**
1 tsp. **Vanilla**
1/3 cup **Butter**

Cream sugar, flour, vanilla and butter together. Sprinkle over surface of apples. Bake for 35 minutes in a 375 degree oven.

1/2 cup **Cream**
1 tsp. **Sugar**
1/2 tsp. **Vanilla**

Combine cream, sugar and vanilla and pour over top of Küchen. Return to oven for 5 minutes.

Grandma's Dried Apple Cake

"My grandmother-in-law brought this recipe from Virginia. She had it memorized. One day I measured the ingredients as she put them out so that I would have a written version. Be sure to read the recipe through before starting!"

Pauline Goldman, Washburn

Filling:

3 cups **Dried Apples**
3 cups **Water**
1/2 cup **Sugar**
1 1/2 tsp. **Allspice**

Dough:

1/3 cup **Shortening**
1/2 cup **Sugar**
2 **Eggs**
1/4 cup **Molasses**
1/4 cup **Buttermilk**
3 cups **Flour**
1 tsp. **Ginger**
1 tsp. **Baking Soda**
1/2 tsp. **Baking Powder**
1/4 tsp. **Salt**

Preheat oven to 475 degrees.

Combine apples and water in a saucepan; bring to a boil and then let apples soak for 4 hours. Mash apples and then stir in sugar and allspice. Set aside.

Cream together the shortening and sugar. Add eggs, molasses and buttermilk. Sift remaining ingredients together and add to the sugar mixture. Knead dough on floured board until semi-stiff. Divide dough into 4 pieces and roll each out to about size of a 9-inch pie pan. Use a plate to trim edges smooth. Places cakes on cookie sheet(s) lined with pastry paper and bake in preheated oven for about 5 minutes, or until light brown. While still hot, place one cake on a platter, top with a cup of apple mixture and repeat with the balance of layers. Cool and wrap tightly. Refrigerate 5 days before serving.

My Mother's Special Devil's Food Cake

"This recipe came from my grandfather's aunt who got it from her mother!"

Bonnie Denis, Green Bay

1/2 cup **Shortening**
3 cups **Dark Brown Sugar**
2 **Eggs,** beaten
2 squares **Cooking Chocolate,** melted
2 1/2 cups sifted **Cake Flour**
1/4 tsp. **Salt**
1/2 cup **Butter**
1/2 tsp. **Vanilla**
1 tsp. **Baking Soda**
1 cup **Boiling Water**

Preheat oven to 350 degrees.

Cream shortening and brown sugar together. Add eggs, chocolate, flour, salt, butter and vanilla. Mix baking soda in boiling water and add to cake mixture. Pour batter into baking pans and bake in preheated oven for 40-45 minutes.

Orange Date Cake

"This is one of my mom's favorite recipes."

Dolores A Haugen, Fond du Lac

3/4 cup **Shortening**
1 3/4 cups **Sugar**, divided
2 **Eggs**, beaten
2 1/2 cups **Flour**
1 tsp. **Baking Powder**
1 cup **Buttermilk**
1 tsp. **Baking Soda**
1 cup chopped **Nuts**
1 1/2 cups chopped **Dates**
Juice of 2 **Oranges**

Preheat oven to 350 degrees.

Cream shortening and 1 cup sugar together. Add eggs and mix well. Sift together the flour and baking powder; combine buttermilk and baking soda. Add flour mixture to egg mixture, alternating with buttermilk. Fold in nuts and dates. Bake in a greased tube pan in preheated oven for 45 minutes. Dissolve remaining 3/4 cup sugar in orange juice. While cake is still hot, poke holes in the top with a fork and pour orange juice over surface. Set cool for 10 minutes before removing cake from pan. Serve with whipped cream or topping.

Schaum Torte

"In German, 'schaum' means 'foam'. This recipe was handed down through generations from my great grandmother. I have continued that tradition by giving it to my granddaughter."

Erma S. Stenzel, West Bend

6 **Egg Whites**
2 cups **Sugar**
1 tsp. **Vanilla**
1 tsp. **Vinegar**
Whipped Cream, to taste
Strawberries, to taste

Preheat oven to 275 degrees.

Beat egg whites until stiff enough to form peaks. Beat in sugar, two tablespoons at a time, 3 times, beating thoroughly after each addition. Beat in vanilla and vinegar and then fold in the remaining sugar. Pour mixture into a greased 10-inch pie pan (or a springform pan) and bake in preheated oven for 1 hour until firm. Leave torte in oven with the door open until cold. Serve, topped with whipped cream and strawberries.

Jelly Roll

2/3 cup pre-sifted **Flour**
1 tsp. **Baking Powder**
3 **Eggs**, beaten
1/2 cup **Sugar**

Filling:

Jam or **Apple Sauce**, as desired

Preheat oven to 425 degrees.

Mix together flour and baking powder. In separate bowl, mix eggs and sugar until white and fluffy. Add flour to egg mixture, stir until well blended. Pour into oblong baking pan lined with buttered waxed paper. Bake in preheated oven for 5 minutes. Turn onto waxed paper sprinkled with sugar, remove bottom paper. Spread with jam or apple sauce. Roll lengthwise. Wrap in waxed paper. Allow to cool. Cut crosswise in slices.

CANDY / FUDGE

Candy/Fudge

Savory scents and winter warmth evoke fond memories of holidays past and the arresting aroma of hot apple pie nudges the German chocolate cake, vying for admiration at center table. But it was Grandma Patty's colorful marzipan that Erin recalls best, crowding the fudge and funny-faced gingerbread men to command the attention it deserved. From apples and bananas to oranges and cherries, Erin's Grandma would spend a whole day before the holidays to create delightful fruit and vegetable imitations from this melt-in-your-mouth confectionery. Every family at the holiday gathering waited impatiently to open gifts, knowing there would be a festive tin of Grandma's magnificent marzipan somewhere in the brightly colored packages.

Chocolate Turtles

1/4 cup **Butter**
1 cup **Evaporated Milk**
1 cup **Sugar**
1 cup **Dark Corn Syrup**
1/4 tsp. **Salt**
1 tsp. **Vanilla**
10 oz. **Pecan Halves**
6 oz. **Semi-Sweet Chocolate Chips**

In small saucepan, heat butter and evaporated milk until butter is melted. In separate 2 quart saucepan, cook sugar, corn syrup and salt over medium heat, stirring often, until it reaches a firm-ball stage at about 244 degrees. Slowly stir in hot milk mixture so that the sugar mixture does not stop boiling. Stir constantly until the candy reaches the firm-ball stage again. Remove pan from heat and stir in vanilla. Cool caramel to room temperature. On waxed paper, arrange 4 pecans and 8 chips per turtle. Place a heaping teaspoon of cooled caramel on top of each group of pecans. Let cool until firm.

Spiced Pecans

2 cups **Sugar**
1/2 cup **Water**
1 1/2 tsp. **Cinnamon**
Pinch of **Salt**
1 tsp. **Vanilla**
2-4 cups **Pecan Halves**

Boil first four ingredients until a soft ball forms. Add vanilla. Stir in pecans. When all are covered, pour onto foil and separate into eating pieces.

Divinity

3 cups **Sugar**
Pinch of **Salt**
2/3 cup **Light Corn Syrup**
2/3 cup **Hot Water**
2 **Egg Whites,** beaten stiffly

Boil sugar, salt and syrup until it cracks in hot water. Slowly pour syrup over egg whites gradually. Beat until thick and loses its gloss. Drop by teaspoonfuls.

Dump Fudge

1/2 cup **Butter**
1 lb. **Powdered Sugar**
1/2 cup **Unsweetened Cocoa**
1/4 cup **Milk**
1 tsp. **Vanilla** or **Rum Extract** or
1/2 tsp. **Mint Extract**
1 cup chopped **Nuts**

In a 9 inch round glass dish microwave butter for 30 seconds on high. Add powdered sugar, cocoa and milk in order given. DO NOT STIR. Microwave 1 1/2 minutes on high. Add extract and nuts. Stir well. Set in refrigerator for 30 minutes.

(Add extra liquid if you want to use this for a frosting.)

Five-Pound Fudge

4 1/2 cups **Sugar**
1 can (12 oz.) **Evaporated Milk**
1/2 lb. **Butter**
18 oz. **Chocolate Chips**
2 cups chopped **Nuts**
3 tsp. **Vanilla**

Mix sugar and milk together and cook for 8 minutes after it begins to boil. Be sure to stir mixture constantly. Mix together butter, chocolate chips, nuts, and vanilla. Add the cooked sugar mixture to the butter mixture. Mix thoroughly. DO NOT BEAT. Pour into large loaf pan to cool. Let set several hours until firm. Slice.

Fudge—Old Fashioned

3 cups **Sugar**
1/2 cup **Milk**
1 cup **Cream**
2 tbsp. **Corn Syrup**
1/4 tsp. **Salt**
2 squares **Semi-Sweet Chocolate**
1 square **Bitter Chocolate**
3/4 tsp. **Vanilla**
3/4 cup **Nuts**

Mix sugar, milk, cream, corn syrup, salt and chocolates. Stir until sugar dissolves and chocolate melts. Cook to 230 degrees on candy thermometer. Take off burner. Cool. Add vanilla, beat until creamy and mixture loses its gloss. Add nuts. Pour into buttered 9 x 9 inch pan. Cool and cut into squares.

Hints to prevent fudge from becoming sugary:

Grease inside of saucepan with butter.

Just before candy comes to a boil, wipe sugar crystals off sides of pan using a small wet cloth wrapped around the tines of a fork.

Never Fail Fudge

1 can (12 oz.) **Evaporated Milk**
1/4 lb. **Butter**
4 cups **Sugar**
12 oz. **Semi-Sweet Chocolate Chips**
1 pint **Marshmallow Creme** or
3 cups **Small Marshmallows**

Place milk, butter, and sugar in saucepan and heat at low temperature (230 degrees F.) until it forms a soft ball, about 6 minutes. Stir often to keep from burning. Remove from heat and fold in the semi-sweet chocolate chips and the marshmallows. Pour into a greased 9 x 12 dish. Cool. Place in the refrigerator.

Fudge Sundae Pie

1 package (6 oz.) **Chocolate Chips**
1 cup **Miniature Marshmallows**
1/4 tsp. **Salt**
1 cup **Evaporated Milk**
1 box **Vanilla Wafers**
1/2 quart **Vanilla Ice Cream**
Chopped **Pecans** or **Walnuts**

Melt chocolate and marshmallows. Mix with salt and milk. Set aside. Butter 10-inch pie plate and line with vanilla wafers. Scoop ice cream over wafers. Pour chocolate mixture over ice cream. Sprinkle top with nuts. Freeze for 12 hours before serving.

Popcorn Balls

1 cup **Sugar**
1/2 tsp. **Salt**
1/3 cup **Molasses**
1 tbsp. **Butter**
2/3 cup **Karo® Light Corn Syrup**
4 quarts **Popped Corn**

Boil first 5 ingredients over low heat to a crack stage. Pour over popped corn and shape into balls.

Chocolate Covered Cherries

3 tbsp. **Butter**
1/4 cup **Evaporated Milk**
1 tsp. **Vanilla**
1/4 tsp. **Salt**
3/4 cups sifted **Powdered Sugar**
48 **Maraschino Cherries**, drained
6 oz. **Semi-Sweet Chocolate Chips**

Melt butter over low heat. Stir in evaporated milk, vanilla and salt. Remove from heat. Gradually stir in sifted powdered sugar. Turn fondant out onto board, lightly sprinkled with powdered sugar; work with hands until smooth. Cover cherries completely by shaping about 2 tsp. fondant around each cherry. Melt semisweet chocolate in double boiler. Drop fondant-covered cherries into melted chocolate to cover. Remove from chocolate with two forks. Place on waxed paper to cool.

Penuche*

4 cups firmly-packed **Brown Sugar**
1/2 cup **Milk** or **Cream**
2 tbsp. **Butter**
1 tbsp. **Vinegar**
1 cup chopped **Pecans**
1 tsp. **Vanilla**

Blend sugar, milk, butter and vinegar; cook until a small amount will form a wax-like ball when dropped in cold water (soft-ball stage, 234 degrees F.). Remove from heat; add vanilla and nut-meats. Stir constantly until it hardens. Spread in buttered pans and cut into squares.

**Penuche is very similar in taste to pralines, though penuche is usually cut into squares. Of course, pecans can be substituted for peanuts in your favorite recipe for nut brittle.*

Apricot Balls

3/4 cup dried **Apricots**
3/4 cup **Flaked Coconut**
1/2 cup chopped **Pecans**
1 tbsp. **Lemon Juice**
1/2 tsp. grated **Lemon Rind**
1/2 tsp. grated **Orange Rind**

Wash and drain apricots; add coconut and pecans. Put through a food grinder. Add lemon juice, lemon and orange rinds. Knead with the hands until well blended. Roll into small balls. If desired, the balls may be rolled in additional chopped pecans. Yields about 3 dozen balls.

Quick, No-Bake Rum Balls

1/2 lb. **Vanilla Wafers**, ground or crushed
1 cup **Powdered Sugar**
2 tbsp. **Cocoa**
1 cup chopped **Pecans**
1/2 cup **Light Corn Syrup**
1/4 cup **Rum**

Combine dry ingredients; add pecans, syrup and rum. Stir until stiff. Coat hands with powdered sugar and roll mixture into balls of desired size. Let stand for about an hour on waxed paper, then roll in additional powdered sugar. Makes about 40.

Fondant*

(Uncooked with Pecans)

1/2 cup (1 stick) **Butter**
2 lbs. **Powdered Sugar**
1 can (14-oz.) **Sweetened Condensed Milk**
1 tbsp. **Vanilla**
2 cups chopped **Pecans**
1 package (6-oz.) melted **Semi-sweet Chocolate Chips**

Mix butter, sugar, milk, vanilla and pecans thoroughly. Roll into small balls; chill 2 hours. Dip balls into melted chocolate. Place balls on waxed paper to cool.

*The name "fondant" comes from the French verb *fondue*, meaning "to melt." A word derived from the French for "sweet tooth" might better suit this candy!

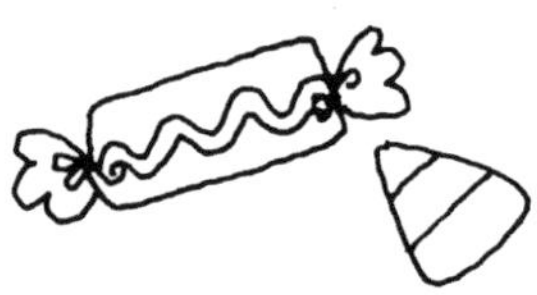

Mom's Breakfast Candy

"This is my mother's homemade candy recipe. To this day it's still a favorite in our family."

Mrs. Ray Marman—Glendive

4 cups **Corn Flakes**
4 cups **Puffed Wheat**
1 cup **Peanuts**
1 cup **Coconut**
1 cup **Karo® Light Corn Syrup**
1 cup **Sugar**
1 cup **Whipping Cream**
Butter

In a large bowl, combine the first four ingredients. In a saucepan, boil syrup, sugar and whipping cream to soft-ball stage. Pour syrup mixture over cereal; mix well. Press into a buttered 13 × 9 pan. When cool, cut into serving size pieces. Do not store in refrigerator.

Lemon Taffy

2 cups **Sugar**
1/4 cup fresh **Lemon Juice**
2 tbsp. **Butter** or **Margarine**
1/4 cup **Water**

Place all ingredients into saucepan and bring to a boil, stirring constantly. Wash down sugar crystals. Continue boiling without stirring, until candy thermometer registers 280 degrees F. or drop a small amount of mixture into ice water. The mixture should separate into hard and brittle threads.

Pour onto greased cookie sheet and let stand until cool enough to handle. Then pull taffy until mixture is white and begins to hold shape. Mold into a rope about 3/4 inch thick. Cut into 1 inch pieces with scissors. Wrap each piece in waxed paper or plastic.

(To prevent hands from becoming sticky while pulling taffy, grease hands with butter.) This recipe makes about a pound of candy.

Strawberry Candy

"This candy is a pretty addition to any Christmas plate."

Mary Redenius—Peoria

2 packages (6 oz. ea.) **Strawberry Jell-O®**
2 cups **Powdered Sugar**
1 can **Eagle Brand® Sweetened Condensed Milk**
2 cups **Coconut Flakes**
1 cup chopped **Nuts**
Red Sugar
Slivered Almonds, colored green

In a bowl, mix all ingredients together except red sugar and almonds. Create strawberry-size shapes. Roll in red sugar and insert a green almond sliver for a stem.

Citrus Gels

1 envelope unflavored **Gelatin**
1 3/4 cups **Orange Juice** (divided)
1/4 cup **Sugar**
1 1/2 cups drained, chilled **Orange** and **Grapefruit Sections**

Sprinkle gelatin over 1/2 cup orange juice in medium saucepan. Place over low heat and stir constantly until gelatin dissolves, about 3 minutes. Remove from heat. Stir in sugar and remaining 1 1/4 cups juice. Chill until consistency of unbeaten egg white. Stir in drained citrus sections and turn into four juice glasses. Chill until set, about 3 hours. Serves 4.

Molasses Candy

1 cup **Sugar**
1 cup **Molasses**
1/4 cup **Butter**
1 cup **Heavy Cream**
1/3 cup coarsely chopped **Almonds**

Mix sugar, molasses, butter and cream together in skillet. Cook over low heat (approximately 250 degrees), stirring constantly until mixture forms soft balls when dropped in cold water. Add almonds and pour in small fluted paper candy cups. Allow to set.

Toffee

2 3/4 cup **Sugar**
1 1/4 cup **Molasses**
2 tbsp. **Cocoa**
3 tbsp. **Butter**
2 1/4 cup **Cream**

Mix all ingredients together; cook on low heat, stirring occasionally until mixture forms soft balls when dropped in cold water. Pour into well-greased oblong pan. Cool slightly. Cut into small squares with greased knife. Wrap in waxed paper to store.

COOKIES

Cookies

Being a kid sometimes isn't all it's cracked up to be. But Grandmas generally have a knack of making things "all better." Scott's Grandma Florence was especially good at that… appearing with fresh-from-the-oven peanut butter cookies at just the right moment… even Ginger their Cocker Spaniel fell under the spell of her delicious chunky cookies. That was obvious the day Ginger followed Scott into Grandma's kitchen to discover the fresh plate of peanut butter cookies, with tasty slivers of almonds, sitting temptingly on the kitchen table. Ginger waited while Scott stuck a couple of cookies into his jacket pocket, grabbed a glass of milk and headed outside. Her head swung first to the left, then to the right, making sure she was alone. Her toenails clicked softly on the tile floor as she crossed to the table and climbed up onto a chair. Scott knew she wouldn't be able to resist, as he peeked in the kitchen window to watch the cookie bandit. Ginger looked around at the door…her front paws raised up and clutched at the maple tabletop, within an inch of the enticing plate of goodies. Her tongue reached out for its reward. "Gin-*ger*!" Grandma Florence whisked into the room and scooped the naughty dog into her arms. But softhearted Grandma couldn't blame Ginger for coveting her peanut butter cookies. She opened the back door and shooed Ginger out, tossing a cookie onto the grass. "Yelp!" was Ginger's muffled thank you as she pounced and gulped it down.

Butterscotch Chip Cookies

1 1/2 cups sifted **Flour**
1 tsp. **Baking Soda**
1/2 cup chopped **Walnuts**
2 cups **Rolled Oats**
1 package (8 oz.) **Butterscotch Chips**
1 cup **Butter**
1/2 cup sifted and packed **Brown Sugar**
1/2 cup **Sugar**
2 **Eggs**, well-beaten
1 tsp. **Vanilla**
1 tsp. **Water**

Preheat oven to 375 degrees.

Mix and sift flour and soda; add nuts, rolled oats and chips. In separate bowl, cream butter well. Add sugars gradually to butter and continue creaming until light and fluffy. Add eggs, vanilla and water to creamed butter mixture. Next, add flour mixture gradually and blend. Drop by spoonful onto baking sheet. Bake in preheated oven for 10 to 11 minutes.

Makes 5 dozen.

Chewy Chocolate Cookies

1 cup softened **Butter or Margarine**
2 cups **Sugar**
2 **Eggs**
2 tsp. **Vanilla**
2 cups unsifted **Flour**
3/4 cup **Hershey's® Cocoa**
1 tsp. **Baking Soda**
1/2 tsp. **Salt**

Preheat oven to 350 degrees.

Cream margarine and sugar in large mixing bowl. Add eggs and vanilla; blend well. Combine flour, cocoa, baking soda and salt; blend into creamed mixture. Drop by teaspoonful onto ungreased cookie sheet. Bake in preheated oven for 8 to 9 minutes. Do not over bake. Cookies will be soft. Cool 1 minute then remove to wire rack. They puff during baking and flatten when cooled.

Makes about 4-1/2 dozen.

Chocolate Oatmeal Cookies

1/4 cup **Butter**
2 cups **Sugar**
1/2 cup **Milk**
1/4 cup **Peanut Butter**
6 tbsp. **Cocoa**
3 cups **Quick Oats**
1 tsp. **Vanilla**

This recipe requires no baking.

Mix butter, sugar and milk together and let boil for 1 minute only. Remove from heat. Add peanut butter and cocoa. Stir until smooth. Add in oats and vanilla; mix well. Drop by spoonful onto waxed paper. Let cool.

Taffy Cookies

"Grandma's cookie tin is always full of these!"

Susan Kolpack, Antigo

1 cup **Brown Sugar**
1 cup **Butter**
1 cup chopped **Pecans**
Graham Crackers, crumbled

Preheat oven to 350 degrees.

Place sugar, butter and pecans in a saucepan and boil for 2 minutes. Line a greased cookie sheet with crumbled graham crackers; pour sugar mixture over all and bake in preheated oven for 10 minutes. Remove from pan immediately, break into cookies and place on waxed paper until cool.

Didi's Meringue Cookies

2 **Egg Whites**
1/2 tsp. **Cream of Tartar**
Pinch of **Salt**
3/4 cup **Sugar**
1 tbsp. **Vanilla**

Preheat oven to 375 degrees.

In mixing bowl, add egg whites, cream of tartar and salt; beat slow to medium until frothy. Next, add sugar and vanilla to egg mixture, one tablespoon at a time, on high speed.

Drop meringue 1 tablespoon at a time onto greased cookie sheet. Place in preheated oven. Turn off oven and leave overnight. Makes approximately 2 dozen cookies.

If desired, chocolate chips, crushed peppermint candy, or nuts may be folded in when vanilla is added.

Frosted Chocolate Cookies

1 3/4 cups **Flour**
1/2 cup **Cocoa**
1 tsp. **Baking Soda**
1/2 tsp. **Salt**
1/2 cup **Butter**

1 cup **Sugar**
2 **Eggs**
1 tsp. **Vanilla**
1/2 cup chopped **Walnuts**
Large **Marshmallows**

Preheat oven to 350 degrees.

Sift first four ingredients. Combine butter, sugar, eggs and vanilla. Next, add flour mixture. Work well with hands. Mix in nuts. Dough will be stiff. Roll dough into balls.

Place in preheated oven for 8 minutes only. DO NOT OVERCOOK.

Cut marshmallows in half. Place cut side down on cookies and return to oven for just 2 minutes longer. Be sure not to overbake. When cool, frost with icing and put nuts on top.

Frosting

3/4 box **Powdered Sugar**
2 tbsp. **Cocoa**

A little **Milk, Vanilla** and **Salt** to taste

Mix into a spreading consistency.

Grandma's Chocolate Chip Cookies

2 cups **Butter**
2 cups **Sugar**
2 cups **Brown Sugar**
4 **Eggs**
2 tsp. **Vanilla**
5 cups **Oatmeal**
4 cups **Flour**
1 tsp. **Salt**
2 tsp. **Baking Powder**
2 tsp. **Baking Soda**
24 oz. **Semi-Sweet Chocolate Chips**
8 oz. **Hershey® Bar**, grated
3 cups chopped **Nuts**

Preheat oven to 350 degrees.

Cream together butter, Sugar, and brown sugar. Add eggs and vanilla to butter-sugar mixture. Put 1/2 cup of oatmeal in a blender and blend until it is a powder. In a separate bowl, mix together the flour, oatmeal (including the oatmeal that was treated in the blender), salt, baking powder and baking soda. Mix together until well blended. Add chocolate chips, grated Hershey® bar, and nuts; mix well. Drop well-rounded tablespoon of dough onto ungreased cookie sheet, 2 inches apart. Bake in preheated oven about 10 to 15 minutes, or until slightly golden.

*When using chocolate chips, use only real chocolate. Chocolate flavored morsels cost less but the taste suffers quite a bit. Use the real deal.

Great-Grandmother's Gingerbread

Recipe is over 100 years old.

1/4 cup **Butter**
1/4 cup **Shortening**
1/2 cup **Sugar**
1 **Egg,** beaten
1 cup **Molasses**
2 1/2 cups sifted **Flour**
1 1/2 tsp. **Baking Soda**
1/2 tsp. **Cloves**
1 tsp. **Cinnamon**
1/2 tsp. **Salt**
1 tsp. ground **Ginger**
1 cup **Hot Water**

Preheat oven to 350 degrees.

Cream butter, shortening and sugar. Add beaten egg and molasses. Next, sift together flour, baking soda, cloves, cinnamon, salt and ginger. Add hot water last and beat until smooth. Bake in greased shallow pan in preheated oven 40-50 minutes. Frost when cool.

Lemon Frosting For Gingerbread

1 3/4 cups **Powdered Sugar**
1/4 cup **Lemon Juice**
1 tbsp. **Cream**
1/8 tsp. grated **Lemon Rind**

Beat until smooth, adding sugar last. Beat to spreading consistency.

Gumdrop Cookies

1 cup **Brown Sugar**
1 cup **Shortening**
1 cup **Sugar**
1 tsp. **Vanilla**
2 **Eggs**
2 cups **Flour**
1 tsp. **Baking Powder**
1/4 tsp. **Salt**
1 tsp. **Baking Soda**
2 cups **Quick Oats**
1 cup cut-up **Gumdrops**
1 cup **Walnuts**

Preheat oven to 350 degrees.

Cream brown sugar, shortening, sugar, vanilla, and eggs. In separate bowl, sift together flour, baking powder, salt, and soda. Add to the creamed mixture. Stir until well mixed. Add the oatmeal, cut-up gumdrops and walnuts. Stir until mixed.

Place rounded spoonfuls onto cookie sheet; bake in preheated oven for 12 to 15 minutes.

Molasses Cookies

1 1/2 sticks **Sweet Butter**
1 cup **Sugar**
1/4 cup **Molasses**
1 **Egg**
1 3/4 cup **Flour**
1/2 tsp. **Cloves**
1/2 tsp. ground **Ginger**
1 tsp. **Cinnamon**
1/2 tsp. **Baking Soda**
Raisins (optional)

Preheat oven to 350 degrees.

Melt butter; add sugar and molasses. Lightly beat egg and add to butter mixture. Mix flour with spices and baking soda. Add to mixture. Raisins may be added, if desired. Batter will be wet. Lay sheet of foil on baking sheet. Drop cookie batter by tablespoon onto foil, leaving 3 inches between cookies. Bake in preheated oven 8 to 10 minutes until cookies start to darken. Remove from oven while still soft. Let cool on foil. Will stay moist in tins for at least a week.

No Bake Cookies

2 cups **Sugar**
1/2 cup **Milk**
2 tbsp. **Butter**
1/2 cup **Peanut Butter**
1 tsp. **Vanilla**
1 cup chopped **Nuts**
4 tbsp. **Cocoa** (add for chocolate)
3 cups **Oats**

In medium saucepan, add sugar, milk, butter and peanut butter; stir over low heat until boiling for 1 minute. Remove from heat. Add remaining ingredients. Stir until well-blended. Drop onto waxed paper. Allow to cool.

The "Best" Oatmeal Cookies

2 **Eggs**, well beaten
1cup **Raisins**
1 tsp. **Vanilla Extract**
1 cup **Butter**
1 cup **Brown Sugar**
1 cup **Sugar**
2 1/2 cups **Flour**
1 tsp. **Salt**
1 tsp. **Ground Cinnamon**
2 tsp. **Baking Soda**
2 cups **Quick Oats**
3/4 cup chopped **Pecans**

Preheat oven to 350 degrees.

Combine eggs, raisins and vanilla. Allow to stand for one hour, covered with plastic wrap. Cream together butter and sugars. Add flour, salt, cinnamon and soda to sugar mixture. Mix well. Blend in egg-raisin mixture, oatmeal and chopped nuts. Dough will be very stiff.

Drop by heaping teaspoons onto ungreased cookie sheet, or roll into small balls and flatten slightly on cookie sheet. Bake in preheated oven for 10 to 12 minutes or until lightly browned.

* The secret…soak the raisins!

Peanut Butter Cookies

1 cup **Shortening**
1 cup softened **Peanut Butter**
1 cup **Sugar**
1 cup packed **Brown Sugar**
2 **Eggs**
1 tsp. **Vanilla**
2 1/2 cups **Flour**
1/2 tsp. **Salt**
1/2 tsp. **Baking Powder**
3/4 tsp. **Baking Soda**

Preheat oven to 375 degrees.

Beat shortening and peanut butter together until creamy. Gradually add sugars, beating thoroughly after each addition. Blend in eggs and vanilla. In separate bowl, mix remaining ingredients and blend into peanut butter mixture. Shape dough into balls about 1 inch diameter. Place 2 inches apart on ungreased baking sheet. Flatten each cookie. Crisscross top of each cookie with a fork.

Bake in preheated oven for 10 to 15 minutes in preheated oven. Remove from baking sheet while warm.

Pecan Crisps

Graham Crackers
1 cup **Brown Sugar**
1/4 lb. **Butter**
1/2 cup **Pecans**

Preheat oven to 325 degrees.

Line buttered 9 x 12 inch pan with whole graham crackers. Boil sugar and butter together for 3 minutes. Pour and spread over graham crackers. Sprinkle with nuts and bake in preheated oven exactly 10 minutes, no longer. Cut into strips or squares when slightly cooled.

Quick Chocolate Chip Cookie Sticks

1/2 cup **Sugar**
1/2 cup packed **Brown Sugar**
1/2 cup **Vegetable Oil**
1 tsp. **Vanilla**
1 **Egg**

1 1/2 cups **Flour**
1/2 tsp. **Baking Soda**
1/2 tsp. **Salt**
1 cup **Chocolate Chips**
1/2 cup chopped **Nuts**

Preheat oven to 375 degrees.

Mix sugars, oil, vanilla and egg in large bowl with spoon until smooth. Stir in flour, baking soda and salt. Divide dough into halves. Shape one half into 2 strips about 15 x 3 inches about 3 inches apart on a lightly greased cookie sheet. Sprinkle each strip with chocolate chips and nuts. Press them down lightly into the dough.

Bake in preheated oven until golden brown, about 7 to 9 minutes. Cool about 2 minutes. Cut each strip crosswise into 1 inch slices. Remove from cookie sheet.

Repeat with remaining dough. Store.

*Keep the size of cookies and strips consistent for even baking.

Raspberry Rolled Cookies

1 cup softened **Butter**
1/2 cup **Sugar**
1 **Egg**
1 tsp. **Vanilla**
2 1/8 cups **Enriched Flour**
1/2 cup **Raspberry Jam**

Preheat oven to 375 degrees.

Melt butter then add to sugar; beat until light and fluffy. Blend in egg and vanilla. Gradually add flour. Mix thoroughly. Divide dough in half. Chill for easier handling (optional).

On lightly floured surface, roll out 1/2 of dough at a time. Spread half of jam on top of dough, covering completely. Roll up dough starting with wide end. Slice cookie 1/4 inch thick. Place cookie on ungreased baking sheet.

Bake in preheated oven 6-9 minutes, or until lightly browned. Cool one minute before removing cookie to plate.

Makes about 4 dozen.

Scrumptious Chocolate Layer Bars

2 cups **Semi-Sweet Chocolate Chips**
8 oz. **Cream Cheese**
2/3 cup **Evaporated Milk**
1 cup chopped **Walnuts**
1 tsp. **Almond Extract**

1 1/2 cups **Sugar**
1 1/2 tsp. **Baking Powder**
1/2 tsp. **Salt**
1 cup softened **Butter**
3 cups **Flour**
2 **Eggs**

Preheat oven to 375 degrees.

Grease 13 x 9 inch pan. Combine chocolate chips, cream cheese and evaporated milk in a medium saucepan. Cook over low heat, stirring constantly until chips are melted and mixture is smooth. Remove from heat. Stir in walnuts and 1/2 tsp. almond extract. Blend well, set aside. Combine remaining ingredients in large mixing bowl. Blend well with mixer until it resembles coarse crumbs. Press half of mixture in pan. Spread with chocolate mixture. Sprinkle rest of crumbs over filling.

Bake in preheated oven for 35 to 40 minutes or until golden brown.

Seven Layer Cookies

2 cups **Graham Cracker Crumbs**
1 1/2 sticks **Margarine**
1 bag (12 oz.) **Chocolate Chips**
1 large bag (14 oz.) **Coconut Flakes**
1 bag (12 oz.) **Butterscotch Chips**
2 cups **Pecans**
1 cup **Milk**

Preheat oven to 350 degrees.

Mix graham cracker crumbs and margarine. Spread evenly over the bottom of 9 x 13 inch baking pan. Layer the chocolate chips, butterscotch chips, coconut, and the pecans over the crust. Pour the milk over the layers. Bake in preheated oven for 30 minutes, or until lightly brown on top and chips are melted. Cool for one hour. Cut into squares.

Sugar Cookies

1 cup **Powdered Sugar**
1 cup **Sugar**
1 cup **Margarine**
1 cup **Vegetable Oil**
2 **Eggs**
1 tsp. **Vanilla**
1 tsp. **Salt**
1 tsp. **Baking Soda**
1 tsp. **Cream of Tartar**
4 cups plus 4 heaping tbsp. **Flour**

Preheat oven to 350 degrees.

Blend powdered sugar, Sugar and margarine. Mix in vegetable oil, eggs, vanilla, salt, baking soda and cream of tarter; then mix in flour. Mix all ingredients well. Make into balls and place on ungreased cookie sheet. Press down with glass dipped in Sugar. Bake in preheated oven for about 10 minutes or until brown around edges.

White Chocolate Cookies

2 lbs. **White Chocolate**
2 cups **Captain Crunch® Peanut Butter Cereal**
2 cups **Rice Krispies**
2 cups **Miniature Marshmallows**, colored
1 cup **Dry Roasted Peanuts**

Melt chocolate on low heat. Mix in other ingredients. Drop by spoonful on waxed paper. Let cool. Store.

Make sure you update cookie sheets so they don't have that dark, years-of-baking look on them. This can burn your cookies. I'm sure you may have nostalgia for Grandma's old baking trays, but go for new and light trays for the best results. If you must use the old ones, then line them with parchment paper.

Finally, wait until your cookies have completely cooled before storing them in air-tight containers at room temperature.

Polish Molasses Cookies

"My grandmother's mother told us that this recipe was over 100 years old. She said that it was brought from Poland in the early 1800s."

Mrs. Stella l. Anderson, Portage

Cream together:

1/2 cup **Molasses**
(either dark or light)
1 **Egg**, well-beaten
1/2 cup **Sugar**
1/4 cup **Hot Water**
1/2 cup **Shortening**

Sift together:

2 1/2 cups **Flour**
1 tsp. **Baking Soda**
2 tsp. **Cinnamon**
1/2 tsp. **Ginger**
Pinch of **Salt**
1 tsp. **Nutmeg**
1 tsp. **Allspice**
1/2 tsp. **Cloves**
1 tbsp. **Cocoa**

Combine creamed and sifted mixtures. Form dough into small balls and place on a cookie sheet about 2 inches apart. Press each with the tines of fork that has been dipped in sugar. When cool, frost cookies with **Whipped Cream Frosting**.

Whipped Cream Frosting

1/4 cup **Flour**
1 cup **Milk**
1/4 cup **Margarine**
1/2 cup **Shortening**
1 cup **Sugar**
2 tsp. **Vanilla**
Pinch of **Salt**

Combine flour and milk in a saucepan and bring to a simmer. Remove from heat and heat thoroughly. Add the balance of ingredients and mix thoroughly again.

Grandma's Chocolate Christmas Cookies

"I remember visiting grandmother Smith when I was young and it was always a treat when she gave me a plate to go down to the cellar to get these cookies she kept in a stone jar."

Matilda "Stormy" Bobula, Baraboo

1 cup **Boiling Water**
8 tbsp. **Cocoa**
2 cups **Shortening**
2 cups **Sugar**
6 **Eggs,** separated
2 cups **Molasses**
8-9 cups **Flour**
2 tsp. **Salt**
2 tsp. **Baking Powder**
2 tsp. **Cloves**
2 tsp. **Nutmeg**
2 tsp. **Cinnamon**

Preheat oven to 375 degrees.

Pour boiling water over cocoa, stir and let cool. Combine cocoa mixture with balance of ingredients (except egg whites) in order listed. Chill dough overnight. Roll out dough and cut out cookies with Christmas cutters. Bake in preheated oven for 10-15 minutes. Use egg whites in your favorite 7-minute Frosting Recipe and frost cookies when cool.

Gudbrandsdal (Gold Band)

"This recipe was first made by my grandmother in Tynset, Norway before she came to the U.S. in the late 1800s."

Borghild Ramseth Nissen, Green Bay

1 cup **Sugar**
1 cup **Butter** or **Margarine**
1 cup **Cornstarch**
2 cups **Flour**
1 cup **Whipping Cream**
1 tsp. **Almond Flavoring**
1 cup slivered **Almonds**

Preheat oven to 250 degrees.

Cream sugar and butter or margarine. Add the rest of ingredients to sugar mixture, blending after each addition. Drop from a tablespoon into greased cookie sheet. Bake in preheated oven for about 1 1/2 hours, or until light brown around the edges (gold band).

Note: This is a no egg, no baking powder recipe. It is very important to bake the cookies long and slow.

Old-Fashioned Sugar Cookies

"My mother, Ruth Evans, used this recipe to make cut-out cookies for every holiday. The large quantity of cookies that this recipe makes reflects the speed at which they disappeared with six kids in the house."

Janice Evans Swanek, Neenah

11 1/4 cups unsifted **Flour**
2 tbsp. **Baking Soda**
2 tsp. **Cream of Tartar**
2 tsp. **Salt**
4 cups **Sugar**
3 cups softened **Margarine**
8 **Eggs**
1 cup **Milk**
2 tbsp. + 2 tsp. **Vanilla**

Preheat oven to 400 degrees.

In a large bowl, sift together the first five ingredients. Cut in margarine until mixture resembles a coarse meal. Blend in eggs, milk and vanilla. Roll dough out on a lightly floured board to 1/16 inch thickness and cut into desired shapes. Bake cookies on ungreased cookie sheet in preheated oven for 6-8 minutes.

Buttermilk Cookies

'These cookies were made by Belgian immigrants to take with them to the fields for a lunch that included milk and cheese. The recipe was given to me by my grandmother."

Kandice S. Bretl, Brussels

3 cups **Sugar**
2 cups **Shortening**
4 **Eggs,** beaten
2 cups **Buttermilk**
2 tbsp. **Vanilla**
2 tsp. **Salt**
3 tbsp. **Baking Powder**
3 tbsp. **Baking Soda**
5 cups **Flour**

Preheat oven to 350 degrees.

Cream sugar and shortening. Add eggs, buttermilk and vanilla. Sift in salt, baking powder and baking soda. Slowly sift in enough flour to make a soft, pliable dough. Chill at least one hour. Roll dough out and cut out cookies with a large cookie or biscuit cutter. Bake in preheated oven for about 15 minutes, or until edges just turn a golden brown.

Sour Cream Sugar Cookies

"The first place I always headed for at my Norwegian grandmother's house was the cookie jar-the next was to my grandma for a big hug."

Bonnie Young, Soldiers Grove

1 3/4 cups **Sugar**
1 cup softened **Butter**
3/4 tsp. **Salt**
4 **Egg Yolks**
2 **Whole Eggs**
1 tsp. **Baking Soda**
2 tbsp. **Hot Water**
1 cup **Sour Cream**
4 cups **Flour**
1 tsp. **Baking Powder**
Sugar

Preheat oven to 350 degrees.

Cream sugar, butter, salt, egg yolks and whole eggs. Dissolve baking soda in hot water and add with the sour cream to sugar mixture. Add and mix the flour and baking powder. Cover and chill for several hours. Roll out dough and cut into large cookies. Sprinkle tops with sugar and bake in preheated oven for 8-10 minutes or until cookies are set.

Walnut Povitica

"My mother came to the U.S. from Croatia n 1904 and she brought this recipe with her. It was baked for her family of fourteen children on every family or holiday occasion."

Catherine M. Delfield-Ashland

2 cups **Milk**
1/2 cup **Butter**
1/2 cup **Sugar**
1 large cake **Yeast**
6 cups **Flour**
4 **Egg Yolks**
3 tsp. **Salt**

Preheat oven to 300 degrees.

Scald milk; add butter and sugar and cool. Dissolve yeast in warm water (about 1/8 cup). Add milk mixture to dissolved yeast. Add 3 cups flour and beat well. Add egg yolks and salt. Add rest of flour and knead until smooth and pliable. Cover and let rise in warm place. When double in size, shake down and let rise in a warm place. Roll out as thin as possible on a floured cloth. Spread with **Walnut Filling.** Roll jelly roll-style and seal ends. Place in a well-greased pan and cover with cloth. Let rise about 15 minutes. Bake in preheated oven for 1 hour. Do not remove from pan until cool.

Walnut Filling

1 1/2 lbs. ground **Walnuts**
1 1/2 cups **Half and Half**
1 cup **Brown Sugar**
1/2 cup **Sugar**
1/2 cup **Honey**
3 tsp. **Cinnamon**
4 tbsp. **Butter**
2 **Eggs**

Combine all ingredients (except eggs) in a saucepan. Bring to a boil, mix well and then cook slightly. Add eggs and beat.

Pecan Fingers

"When I was a child, my grandmother, Betty Vesperman, made these cookies at Christmastime."

Samantha Buergi, Green Bay Area Visitor and Convention Bureau, Green Bay

1 cup **Butter**
1/4 cup **Brown Sugar**
2 cups **Flour**
1/2 tsp. **Salt**
1 tbsp. **Water**
1 tsp. **Vanilla**
2 cups chopped **Pecans**
Powdered Sugar, as needed

Preheat oven to 350 degrees.

Cream butter and sugar well. Add flour, salt, water and vanilla. Stir in pecans and beat. Roll dough out into finger size rolls and cut into 3-inch lengths. Bake in preheated oven for 18-20 minutes. While still warm, roll cookies in powdered sugar.

Macaroons

1 1/3 cup **Almonds**
1 1/2 cup **Powdered Sugar**
2 **Egg Whites**

Preheat oven to 325 degrees.

Grind almonds; place in mixing bowl. Add sugar. Work mixture until smooth and firm, adding egg whites gradually. Drop teaspoonfuls on well-greased and floured cookie sheets or force mixture through fluted pastry tube in rings, tops and other shapes. Decorate with strips of candied orange peel, cherries and nuts. Bake in preheated oven until light yellow (for approximately 30 minutes). Makes approx. 20-30 cookies

Bruce's Grandma Hannah's cheery voice would snap him to attention when she said, "Bruce, I need some fresh lemons!" He knew that when he returned from her big back yard full of all kinds of good-smellin' fruits and vegetables, and set the basket full of the plumpest, ripest lemons on the kitchen table, there would be eight shiny quarters waiting for him. Best of all, soon, the kitchen was filled with Grandma's happy, tuneful humming and the lemon-fresh aroma of "yellow egg-bread." That's all he ever heard it called…and he swears it's the best bread he has ever tasted. Problem is, he has never found anything like it in any bakery and that's the one recipe you won't see here. Wonder if it had potatoes in it?

FROSTING
Milk
Sugar
Vani
BUTTER

Frosting

Vanilla Frosting

1 cup **Milk**
5 tbsp. **Flour**
Pinch of **Salt**
1/2 cup **Butter**
1/2 cup **Shortening**
1 cup **Sugar**
2 tsp. **Vanilla**

Cook the milk, flour and salt over medium heat until thick. Let the mixture cool. Beat together butter, shortening and sugar, until creamy. Add the vanilla. Add the cooked, cooled custard-like mixture and beat until creamy. Spread over cooled cake.

Cream Cheese Frosting

2 cups **Powdered Sugar**
8 oz. **Cream Cheese**, softened
1 tbsp. **Vanilla**
1 tbsp. **Milk**

Add all ingredients together. Beat until smooth. Spread.

Orange Butter Frosting

1/2 cup packed **Brown Sugar**
1/4 cup **Butter**
1 1/3 tbsp. grated **Orange Peel**
1 tbsp. fresh **Orange Juice**
1 cup **Shredded Coconut**
1/2 cup chopped **Nuts**

In a saucepan, combine brown sugar, butter, orange peel and orange juice. Bring to boil and cook 1 minute, stirring constantly. Stir in coconut and nuts. Set aside to cool.

Fluffy Lemon Frosting

1/2 cup softened **Butter**
Dash of **Salt**
4 cups sifted **Powdered Sugar**
3 tbsp. **Lemon Juice**
2 tsp. **Lemon Peel**

Combine butter and salt in a bowl and beat until smooth. Add a few tablespoons of powdered sugar to butter mixture and continue beating. Add remaining sugar alternately with lemon juice and peel. Continue beating until light and fluffy.

Boiled Brown Sugar Frosting

2/3 cup packed **Brown Sugar**
4 tbsp. **Butter**
1/3 cup **Evaporated Milk**
2 cups **Powdered Sugar**
1 tbsp. **Vanilla**

In a saucepan, bring the first three ingredients to a boil. Remove from heat and cool slightly. Place mixture in a mixer bowl and add powdered sugar and vanilla. Beat until thick enough to spread.

Whipped Cream Frosting

Mrs. Stella l. Anderson—Portage

1/4 cup **Flour**
1 cup **Milk**
1/4 cup **Margarine**
1/2 cup **Shortening**
1 cup **Sugar**
2 tsp. **Vanilla**
Pinch of **Salt**

Combine flour and milk in a saucepan and bring to a simmer. Remove from heat and stir thoroughly. Add the balance of ingredients and mix thoroughly again.

Maple Icing

Susan Kolpack—Antigo

1 cup **Maple Syrup**
2 **Egg Whites,** stiffly beaten

Boil maple syrup until it spins a thin thread. Add slowly to egg whites and beat until stiff.

Marshmallow-Pineapple Frosting

Catherine Zehren Mueller—De Pere

1 tbsp. **Lemon Juice**
1/3 cup **Pineapple Juice**
1 package (10 oz.) **Marshmallows** (quartered)
1 cup **Heavy Cream**

Combine lemon and pineapple juices, add quartered marshmallows and let soak for 3-4 hours. Whip cream until stiff and fold in along with marshmallows.

Almond Icing

Lori Spindler, Warrens Cranberry Festival—Warrens

1 tsp. **Butter**
2 tbsp. **Milk**
1 1/2 cups **Powdered Sugar**
1/2 tsp. **Almond Extract**

In a small glass bowl, combine butter and milk. Microwave on high for 30-45 seconds until hot. Add powdered sugar and almond extract; stir until smooth.

Have you ever noticed that Grandmas – it seems nearly all of them – make it their business to encourage their grandchildren to strive for the best? It was this quality in Todd's Grandma Sharon that forced him to learn how to make a perfect crepe. "I can't," he whined. "There's no such word as 'can't,'" was her retort. Well, there *hadn't* been in her day...but that's a different issue. Point is, she would not let him get away with quitting. On his eighth try, he finally mastered the proper pan heat and "the flip." Todd can now turn a crepe or omelet to perfection, thanks to his Grandma's faith that he could. (The first seven made tasty, but messy meals!)

ICE CREAM

Ice Cream

When Tammy's Grandma wasn't frittering with her corn fritters, she was making something crafty for someone special (like Tammy!), or…you guessed it…the kitchen! "Store bought" only worked for her Grandma Sally when it came to food. Everything else was better made by hand. Tammy said, "Her hand-sewn kitchen curtains trimmed in blue crocheted lace and cross-stitched with a gaggle of baby geese trailing after the momma are better than any ol' geometric design from the mall. Don't you think?"

Ice Cream—Vanilla

3 **Eggs**
1 1/2 cups **Milk**
3/4 cup **Sugar**
1 cup **Whipped Cream**
1 tbsp. **Vanilla**

Cook eggs, milk and sugar in double boiler until custard coats spoon. Cool. Add whipped cream and vanilla. Place in freezer container and freeze. Makes 2 quarts.

Ice Cream—Chocolate

5 **Eggs**
1/2 cup **Sugar**
1 or 2 boxes of **Chocolate Junket® Ice Cream Mix**
1 pint + 1 cup **Half & Half**
1/2 pint **Heavy Whipping Cream**
1 tbsp. **Vanilla**
1/2 tsp. **Lemon Juice**
2-3 quarts **Milk**

In a large mixing bowl, beat eggs lightly, add sugar, Junket®, and 1 cup half & half. Add heavy cream, remaining half and half, vanilla, and lemon juice. Pour into 1-gallon ice cream freezer. Fill container to fill line with milk and freeze. Makes a light chocolate.

(For vanilla ice cream, use vanilla Junket® powder.)

Fudgsicles

1 package **Chocolate Pudding**
1/3 cup **Sugar**
1 cup **Milk**

Cook 1 package chocolate pudding. Mix as directed. Add sugar and milk. Pour into molds and freeze.

Popsicles

2 cups **Hot Water**
1 package (6 oz.) **Jell-O®** (any flavor)
1 package **Kool-Aid®** (same flavor as Jell-O®)
1 cup **Sugar**
2 cups **Cold Water**

Add the hot water to the first 3 ingredients; then add the cold water. Mix. Put in popsicle containers and freeze.

Citrus Sundae

2 cup **Orange Sections** (or **Tangerine Sections**) drained
1/4 cup **Orange-Flavored Liqueur**
1 pt. **Vanilla Ice Cream**
1 pt. **Orange Sherbet**

In a shallow, leakproof covered container, marinate the orange or tangerine sections in the liqueur for a day. Turn container upside down once during the period.

At serving time, scoop a ball of ice cream and one of sherbet into each individual serving dish. Top with oranges and marinade. Serves 6.

Blueberry Ice Cream

1 envelope **Unflavored Gelatin**
1/2 cup **Cold Milk**
1/2 cup **Boiled Milk**
2 cups fresh **Blueberries**
3/4 cup **Sugar**
2 cups whipped **Heavy Cream**

In a 5-cup blender, sprinkle unflavored gelatin over cold milk. Let stand 3-4 minutes. Add hot milk and process at low speed until gelatin is completely dissolved, about 2 minutes. Let cool completely. Add blueberries and sugar, processing at a high speed until blended. Pour into a large bowl and chill, stirring occasionally, until mixture mounds slightly when dropped from a spoon. Fold whipped cream into gelatin mixture. Pour into two 4 × 10 freezer trays or an 8-inch baking pan. Freeze until firm.

Makes 1 1/2 quarts.

Ol' Time Ice Cream

3 **Eggs**, beaten
1 1/2 cups **Milk**
3/4 cup **Sugar**
1 cup **Whipped Cream**
1 tbsp. **Vanilla**

Cook eggs, milk and sugar in a double boiler, stirring frequently, until custard coats spoon; cool to 80 degrees. Add whipped cream and vanilla. Pour mixture into the can of an ice cream freezer and freeze according to manufacturer's directions. Makes 2 quarts.

Ice Cream Baked Potato

Ellis Walker—Boise

Vanilla Ice Cream
Sweetened Cocoa Powder
Whipped Cream
Oreo® Cookies, crumbled
Nuts, chopped
Maraschino Cherries

Let ice cream soften enough to be worked with your hands. Form into the shape of a baking potato, place on waxed paper and return to freezer to harden. Remove and roll frozen 'potatoes' in cocoa powder. Cut open, like a baked potato. Fill with whipped cream, top with crumbled cookies, nuts and cherries.

Peanut Butter Ice Cream

"This is a favorite with ice cream lovers!"

Gloria J. Moore—Gloria's Coffee and Quilts, Barnes

4 large **Eggs**
2 cups **Sugar**
2 cups chunky **Peanut Butter**
2 cups **Cream**
2 tbsp. **Vanilla**
1/2 tsp. **Salt**
2-3 quarts **Milk**

In a large bowl, beat eggs until frothy. Mix in sugar and peanut butter. Add cream, vanilla and salt to mixture; blend well. Pour into a 1-gallon ice cream freezer. Fill container to fill line with milk and freeze per freezer directions.

Some cooks raise their wooden spoon in anger if you add to, top, or mix their creation with a condiment or superfluous ingredient not in their recipe. But in Gary's family, Grandma Tess had to be tolerant, as someone was always experimenting with tastes. Grandpa George first instilled the cooking wanderlust in Gary when he topped one of Grandma's fluffy waffles...not with good ol' sticky maple syrup, but...with creamy, stick-to-the-roof-of-your-mouth peanut butter! It melted right down into the hot waffle's craters and created a whole new taste for Gary that propelled him towards becoming a master chef. Mmmmmm...mmmmm! That day, Grandma just sat down between Gary and Grandpa, shaking her head, and drowned her waffle in syrup.

PIES

Pies

Cooking is so much easier today; with automated appliances and techno-gadgets that seem to require little effort. Except for baking. Yes, you can buy your goodies ready to pop in the oven, or simply open the plastic container. But for the pleasure *and* the taste of it, baking from scratch is still best and there is no high-tech, new-fangled widget that replaces the rolling pin. Rolling dough for pies, cookies, and turnovers are some of Donnie's fondest memories in the kitchen. An easy kid-task is rolling the dough. Can't get into much trouble…right? Well, his Grandma Judy left to do some laundry and set him to work rolling dough for a pumpkin pie. Daydreaming, Donnie soon became Darth Vader and jabbed his saber sword in the air, spinning around to fend off another attack. Unfortunately, Vader turned into Grandma and he nearly took off her head. Needless to say, he was suspended from rolling pin duty for a while…but he still has that old roller displayed in his kitchen.

Apple Pie—Dutch

1 unbaked (9 inch) **Pie Shell**
2/3 cup unsifted **All-Purpose Flour**
1/3 cup **Butter**
1/3 cup **Light Brown Sugar**
2 **Tart Cooking Apples**
1 tbsp. **Lemon Juice**
2 tbsp. **Flour**
3/4 cup **Sugar**
Dash of **Salt**
1 tsp. **Cinnamon**

Preheat oven to 400 degrees.

Prepare pie shell. Refrigerate until ready to use.

Topping:

Combine 2/3 cup flour, butter and brown sugar in medium bowl. With pastry blender or 2 knives, cut in until mixture is consistency of coarse cornmeal. Refrigerate.

Filling:

Core and pare apples. Slice thinly into large bowl. Sprinkle with lemon juice. Combine 2 tbsp. flour, sugar, salt and cinnamon, mixing well. Toss lightly with apples. Turn filling into unbaked pie shell, spread evenly. Cover with topping.

Bake in preheated oven 40 to 45 minutes, or until apples are tender.

Apple Pie—Paper Bag

1 unbaked (9 inch) **Pie Shell**
3 or 4 large (about 2 1/2 lbs.) **Baking Apples**
1/2 cup **Sugar** (for filling)
1/4 cup **Flour** (for filling)
1/2 tsp. **Nutmeg**
1/2 tsp. **Cinnamon**
2 tbsp. **Lemon Juice**
1/2 cup **Sugar** (for topping)
1/2 cup **Flour** (for topping)
1/2 cup **Butter** or **Margarine**

Preheat oven to 425 degrees.

Pare, core and slice apples. Place in large bowl. Combine sugar, flour and spices in bowl for filling and then sprinkle over apples. Toss to coat well and spoon into pastry shell. Drizzle with lemon juice. Combine remaining sugar and flour in small bowl. Cut in butter or margarine and sprinkle over apples covering top.

Slide pie into heavy brown paper bag, large enough to cover pie loosely. Fold open end over twice and fasten with paper clips. Place on cookie sheet for easier handling. Bake in preheated oven for 1 hour.

Split bag open, remove pie and serve. It is delicious warm with ice cream.

This is good for any fruit pie and when done it is a golden brown. Never fails.

Apple Torte

Crust:

1 **Egg**
1/3 cup **Sugar**
1/4 cup **Milk**
2 cups **Enriched Flour**
1 tsp. **Baking Powder**
1 tsp. **Salt**

Filling:

2 large **Apples**
1 **Egg**
1/4 cup **Sugar**
2 tbsp. **Evaporated Milk**

Preheat oven to 400 degrees.

Butter a 9 or 10 inch round baking pan. Place 1 egg, 1/3 cup sugar and milk in a medium sized mixing bowl and beat until blended. Sift together flour, baking powder and salt. Gradually stir in egg mixture to form soft dough that can be handled. Place dough in prepared baking pan and pat dough to cover the bottom and sides. To prepare filling, peel and slice apples. Arrange them on dough, overlapping the slices. Beat together egg, 1/4 cup sugar and evaporated milk in small bowl. Drizzle mixture over apples. Bake in preheated oven for 25 to 30 minutes.

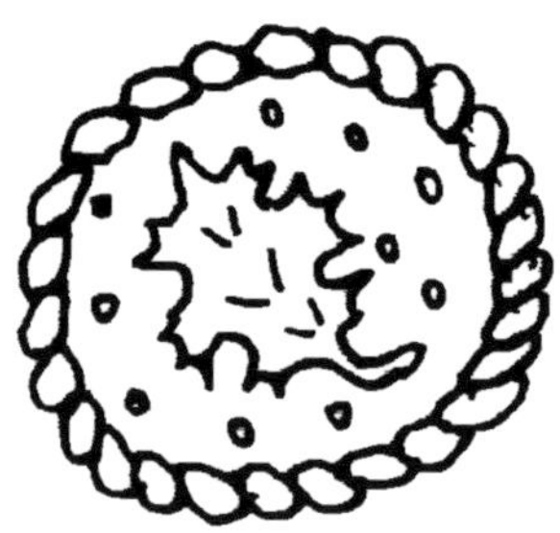

Black Bottom Pie

1 1/2 cup fine **Graham Cracker Crumbs**
1/4 cup **Sugar**
1/3 cup melted **Butter**
1 tbsp. **Unflavored Gelatin**
1/4 cup **Cold Water**
1 cup **Sugar**
1/2 tsp. **Salt**
1/4 cup **Cornstarch**
2 cups **Milk**
4 **Eggs**, separated
6 oz. **Semisweet Chocolate Pieces**
1 tsp. **Vanilla**
1/4 cup **Golden Rum**
1/4 tsp. **Cream of Tartar**
1/2 cup whipped **Heavy Cream**
Chocolate Curls, optional

Preheat oven to 350 degrees.

Using fork, mix crumbs and 1/4 cup sugar in medium bowl; add butter and mix thoroughly. Pat mixture on bottom and side of a 9-inch pie plate. Bake in preheated oven 8 minutes. Cool. Sprinkle gelatin over 1/4 cup cold water to soften. In saucepan, combine 1/2 cup sugar, salt, cornstarch and gradually stir in milk. Bring to boiling, stirring until thickened. In small bowl, beat egg yolks slightly; gradually stir in half of the hot mixture and pour back into saucepan. Return custard to heat; cook, stirring, 2 minutes. Remove saucepan from heat; measure 1/2 cup of custard. Add chocolate pieces and vanilla; stir until chocolate is melted; pour into pie shell. Refrigerate 45 minutes.

Add gelatin to remaining custard, stirring until gelatin dissolves. Cool to lukewarm. Add rum and refrigerate. In medium bowl, add egg whites and cream of tartar; beat until soft peaks form. Gradually beat in remaining 1/2 cup sugar, 2 tbsp. at a time, beating until stiff. Fold whites into rum-flavored custard; pour over chocolate mixture.

Refrigerate at least 6 hours. Garnish with rosettes of whipped cream and chocolate curls.

Cherry Cheese Pie

9 inch **Graham Cracker Pie Crust** or Baked **Pastry Shell**
8 oz. **Cream Cheese**, softened
1 can (14 oz.) **Sweetened Condensed Milk**
1/3 cup **Concentrated Lemon Juice**
1 tsp. **Vanilla**
1 can (21 oz.) **Cherry Pie Filling**, chilled

In a large mixing bowl, beat cheese until fluffy. Gradually beat in sweetened condensed milk until smooth. Stir in lemon juice and vanilla. Pour into prepared crust.

Chill 3 hours or until set. Top with desired amount of pie filling before serving. Refrigerate leftovers.

Chocolate Chip Torte

2 **Egg Yolks**
2 1/2 tbsp. **Sugar**
2/3 cup **Milk**
Dash of **Salt**
1/2 tsp. **Vanilla**
1 tbsp. **Unflavored Gelatin**
2 **Egg Whites**, beaten stiffly
1/4 cup **Cold Water**
1/2 cup coarsely chipped **Semi-Sweet Chocolate**
1 cup whipped **Heavy Cream**
1 **Graham Cracker Pie Crust**

Beat egg yolks and sugar. Add milk and salt. Cook in double boiler until thick, stirring constantly. Add vanilla, and gelatin softened in water. Chill until partially set. Fold in egg whites, beaten with remaining sugar. Fold in chocolate chips. Pour into graham cracker crust. Chill until firm. Serve with whipped cream.

Chocolate Éclair Torte

Crust:

1 cup **Water**
1/2 cup **Margarine** or **Butter**
1/4 tsp. **Salt**
1 cup **Flour**
4 **Eggs**

Filling:

2 packages (3 1/2 oz. each) **Instant French Vanilla Pudding**
2 1/4 cups **Milk**
1 tsp. **Vanilla Extract**
1 container (12 oz.) **Cool Whip® Whipped Topping**

Glaze:

2 squares **Unsweetened Chocolate**
3 tbsp. **Butter**
3 tbsp. **Milk**
1 tsp. **Vanilla**
1 cup **Powdered Sugar**

Preheat oven to 400 degrees.

In a saucepan combine water, margarine and salt. Bring to a boil and cook until margarine is melted. Remove from heat. Add flour to pan all at once and stir to blend. Beat in eggs, one at a time. Spread as evenly as possible in a greased and floured 9 x 13 inch pan. Bake in preheated oven for 45 to 50 minutes or until golden brown. Cool. While crust is warm and not sunken in on itself, lift it carefully and place it on a flat surface. With a long, sharp knife cut it into 2 layers. Return bottom layer to original pan; place top layer on a platter.

Prepare the filling by combining the pudding, milk and vanilla and stirring until it thickens. Fold in Cool Whip®. Spread the filling over bottom layer. Replace top layer gently.

For glaze, melt the chocolate and butter in a small pan. Transfer mixture to a medium size bowl. Add milk, vanilla and sugar. Blend well. With a spoon, drizzle the glaze over the top layer in a lacy pattern.

Delicious Pumpkin Pie

8 oz. **Cream Cheese**, room temperature
1/2 cup firmly packed **Light Brown Sugar**
2 large **Eggs**
2/3 cup canned **Solid-Packed Pumpkin**
3/4 tsp. **Pumpkin Pie Spice**
1unbaked (8-inch) **Graham Cracker Crust**
Cool Whip® Whipped Topping, optional

Preheat oven to 350 degrees.

Beat together cream cheese, sugar and eggs. Add pumpkin and spice. Pour in crust. Bake in preheated oven for 35 minutes. Top with Cool Whip® when served if desired.

Easy Apple Pie

3 **Apples**
2 tbsp. **Butter** (for pan)
3 tbsp. **Water**
3 tbsp. **Sugar**
Dash of **Cinnamon**
1/2 cup **Butter**
1 cup **Brown Sugar**
1 cup **Flour**
1/2 tsp. **Salt**

Preheat oven to 350 degrees.

Slice apples and place in buttered pan, about 8 x 11 inches. Add the water, sugar and cinnamon. Cream the butter and brown sugar and add flour and salt to make a paste. Spread paste over apples and bake in preheated oven for 1 hour. Serve with whipped cream or ice cream.

Easy Lemon Pie

1 can (8 oz.) **Frozen Lemonade Concentrate**
1 container (12 oz.) **Cool Whip® Whipped Topping**
1 can (14 oz.) **Condensed Milk**
1 **Graham Cracker Crust**

Mix undiluted lemonade, whip cream, and milk. Pour into crust. Refrigerate until ready to serve.

Grandma's Chocolate Pie

3 tbsp. **Flour**
4 tbsp. **Cocoa**
1 cup **Sugar**
1 tsp. **Vanilla**
2 **Eggs**, separated
2 cups **Milk**
1 baked (9 inch) **Pie Shell**
Frozen Whipped Topping, thawed

Mix flour, cocoa, sugar, vanilla, egg yolks and a small amount of milk in saucepan. Mix well and then add remaining milk. Cook until thick, stirring constantly. Pour into baked pie shell. Brown in oven. Cool and cover with whipped topping.

Lime Pie

1 can (14 oz.) **Condensed Milk**
1/4 tsp. **Salt**
1/4 cup **Unsweetened Lime Juice**
1 can (8 oz.) **Crushed Pineapple**, well drained
Green Food Coloring, if desired
1 baked (8-inch) **Pie Shell**
Whipped Cream or **Toasted Coconut**, for garnish

Pour milk into heavy saucepan, stir in salt and lime juice. Stir until very thick. Add pineapple and coloring. Pour into pie shell. Chill until firm. Garnish with whipped cream and/or toasted coconut.

Pie Crust— Flaky

4 cups **Flour**
2 tsp. **Salt**
1 tsp. **Baking Powder**
1 1/2 cups **Shortening**
1 **Egg**
1 tbsp. **White Vinegar**
1/2 cup **Cold Water**

Sift together flour, salt and baking powder. Cut in shortening. Beat egg. Add vinegar and water to it. Gradually add liquid to flour mixture and combine. Add a little more water if needed. Divide dough into quarters. Wrap in waxed paper and refrigerate until ready to use.

Pumpkin Pie Filling—Canned

1 can (15 oz.) **Pumpkin**
1/2 can (14 oz.) **Evaporated Milk**
2 cups **Sugar**
4 tsp. **Pumpkin Pie Spice**
6 **Eggs**, beaten
1/4 tsp. **Salt**
1 tsp. **Lemon extract**
3 unbaked (9 inch) **Pie Shells** or
2 unbaked (11 inch) **Pie Shells**

Preheat oven to 350 degrees.

Mix all ingredients together. Pour into unbaked pie shells. Bake in preheated oven for 1 hour.

Makes 3 - 9 inch pies or 2 - 11 inch pies.

Pumpkin Pie Filling—Fresh

3 cups of diced **Fresh Pumpkin**
1/2 tsp. **Salt**
1 1/2 cups **Sugar**
1 heaping tsp. **Cinnamon**
1 tsp. **Allspice** or **Pumpkin Pie Spice**
3 **Eggs**
3 1/2 cups **Milk**
2 unbaked (9-inch) **Pie Shells**

Preheat oven to 425 degrees.

Boil pumpkin with salt and enough water to cover for about 1/2 hour until soft. Strain and mash immediately. Add sugar, cinnamon and allspice. Blend in well-beaten eggs and milk. Pour mixture into 2 unbaked pie shells and bake in preheated oven at least 45 minutes.

Rhubarb Pie

3 cups diced **Rhubarb**, 1inch pieces
1 1/2 cups **Sugar**
2 **Eggs**, beaten
1/2 tsp. **Salt**
2 heaping tbsp. **Flour**
1 1/2 tbsp. **Butter** or **Margarine**

Preheat oven to 425 degrees. Mix diced rhubarb and sugar well; add beaten eggs, salt and flour. Make pastry for two-crust pie.* Pour into pastry-lined pie pan. Dot with butter. Cover with top crust, which has slits cut in it.

Cover edge with 1 1/2" strip of aluminum foil to prevent excessive browning. Bake in preheated oven for 20 minutes, then lower temperature to 350 degrees for about 30 to 40 minutes, until nicely browned.

*See Pie Crust, Flaky, pg. 100.

Strawberry Pudding Pie

1 small **Banana**
1 pint **Strawberries**
1 cup **Cold Milk**
1 package (3 oz.) **Instant Banana** or **Vanilla Pudding Mix**
1 tbsp. grated **Orange Peel**
1 1/2 cup **Frozen Whipped Topping**, thawed
1 baked (9-inch) **Pie Shell**

Arrange sliced banana and 1/2 of the strawberries in bottom of pie shell. Mix cold milk and pudding mix in a bowl. Beat with wire whisk for 1 minute. Fold in rind and whipped topping. Spoon into pie shell over fruit. Garnish with remaining strawberries. You can brush with melted apple or berry jelly.

Sweet Potato Pie

2 (9 inch) **Deep Dish Pie Shells**
3 1/2 cups cooked mashed **Sweet Potatoes**
(3 to 4 large **Sweet Potatoes**)
1/2 cup softened **Butter or Margarine**
2 cups **Sugar**
4 **Eggs**
2 tsp. **Nutmeg**
1 tsp. **Mace** (optional)
1/2 tsp. **Salt**
1 can (13 oz.) **Evaporated Milk**

Preheat oven to 425 degrees.

Bake or boil sweet potatoes until done. If baked, cool slightly and scoop out potato. If potatoes are boiled, remove them from the water immediately after cooking and drain them in a colander. Cool, peel, and mash the potatoes and place them in a large bowl. Stir in butter and sugar. Add eggs. Beat well. Add nutmeg, mace, salt, and milk. Mix well. Pour into pie shells. Bake in preheated oven for 20 minutes. Reduce temperature to 325 degrees and bake for 30 to 45 minutes longer. Knife inserted in center should come out clean.

Rhubarb Dessert

"This was my grandmother's recipe."

Kathy Kuderer, Down A Country Road Bed & Breakfast, Cashton

Crust:

1 cup **Flour**
1/2 cup **Butter**
5 tbsp. **Powdered Sugar**

Topping:

1 1/2 cups **Sugar**
2 **Eggs,** beaten
1/4 cup **Flour**
3/4 tsp. **Salt**
2 cups chopped **Rhubarb**

Preheat oven to 350 degrees.

Add crust ingredients to a medium-sized bowl and, using a pastry blender, blend to the size of small peas. Press mixture into an ungreased 7 1/2 x 11 baking pan and bake for 15 minutes at 350 degrees. Combine topping ingredients and pour into crust. Bake in preheated oven for 35 minutes.

Grandmother's Apple Crisp

"My grandmother was born, raised and lived in Wisconsin until her death at the age of 94. I have lived in Wisconsin all of my 62 years. Grandmother shared this recipes with me in 1956. It is easy to make and a wonderful delight to eat."

Sally Blair, Hudson

6 to 8 small **Apples**, peeled and cored
1/4 cup **Water**
1 1/2 tsp. **Cinnamon**
Pinch of **Salt**

Topping:

1 cup **Sugar**
3/4 cup **All-Purpose Flour**
1/3 cup **Butter**
Whipped Cream or **Ice Cream** of choice

Preheat oven to 350 degrees.

Butter a 9-inch pie plate. Cut apples into 1/2-inch slices and place in pie plate. Pour water over apples and sprinkle with half of the cinnamon and a small pinch of salt. To make the topping; using a pastry blender, mix together sugar, flour, butter and remaining cinnamon until butter is cut to the size of small peas. Sprinkle mixture over apples and, using your hands, pat down lightly. Place pie plate on a foil-lined baking sheet. Bake in preheated oven for 45 to 50 minutes, until apples are tender and top is nicely browned. Serve warm with whipped cream or ice cream.

Lemon Meringue Pie

"My 90-year-old mother-in-law is still winning blue ribbons at the Choteau County Fair for this delicious pie!"

Donna Smith—Kalispell, MT

1 cup **Sugar**
3 heaping tbsp. **Cornstarch**
4 **Egg Yolks**, beaten
1 **Lemon**, juiced with pulp
2 cups **Boiling Water**
1 tbsp. **Butter**
1 baked (9-inch) **Pie Shell**

Preheat oven to 375 degrees.

In a bowl, combine sugar and cornstarch; add egg yolks, lemon juice and pulp. Cook over low heat until sugar is dissolved. Add water slowly, stirring constantly and cook until mixture has thickened and is clear. Remove from heat; add butter. While hot, pour into pie shell. Mound Meringue on top, spreading to edges and bake in preheated oven until meringue is golden brown.

Meringue

4 **Egg Whites**
1/4 tsp. **Cream of Tartar**
1/2 cup **Sugar**

Add egg whites to a bowl, stir in cream of tartar and then gradually add and beat in sugar until soft peaks form and sugar is completely dissolved.

Blueberry Pie

Crust:

1 2/3 cups pre-sifted **Flour**
1 cup cold, unsalted **Butter**
4 tbsp. **Ice Water**

Filling:

1 quart **Blueberries**
3/4 cup **Sugar**

Preheat oven to 425 degrees.

In mixing bowl, add flour, fold in butter. Gradually add water and work dough until mixed. Chill mixture for 30 minutes. Roll out to a rectangular shape on floured baking board, fold; repeat 2 or 3 times and chill again. Repeat this procedure twice. Wash and drain berries. Place in a bowl, sprinkle with sugar and allow to stand.

Divide dough into two portions. Roll out one portion and cover bottom of deep pie plate. Prick surface with fork to remove air bubbles and bake in preheated oven 10-15 minutes or until almost baked, then chill. Roll out remaining dough, line sides of plate, pressing to bottom. Fill pastry shell with blueberries, placing one strip around the edge. Brush with a beaten egg and bake at 425 degrees for 20 minutes or until golden brown. Serve with Vanilla Sauce or cream.

Vanilla Sauce

3 **Egg Yolks,** beaten
2 tbsp. **Sugar**
1 cup heated **Cream**
2 tsp. **Vanilla Extract**
3/4 cup **Whipped Cream**

In double boiler, add beaten egg yolks and sugar. Add heated cream and cook until thick, stirring constantly. Remove from heat; add vanilla and cool, beating occasionally. When cold, fold in whipped cream and serve with your favorite dessert.

PUDDING

Pudding

Black Bottom Pudding

1 1/2 tsp. **Unflavored Gelatin**
1/4 cup **Cold Water**
2 cups **Milk**
4 **Eggs**, separated
1/2 cup **Sugar**, divided
2 tsp. **Cornstarch**
1 oz. **Unsweetened Chocolate**, melted
1 tsp **Vanilla**
3 tbsp. **Dark Rum**
1/4 tsp. **Cream of Tartar**
Chocolate Curls, for garnish

In small bowl sprinkle gelatin over water; set aside. In medium saucepan scald milk. In small bowl beat egg yolks. Slowly whisk in hot milk. Stir in 1/4 cup sugar and cornstarch.

In top of double boiler cook egg mixture over hot, not boiling, water, stirring frequently 20 minutes or until custard thickly coats a spoon. Remove 1-cup custard and stir in chocolate and vanilla until well blended; set aside. Add softened gelatin to remaining custard in double boiler. Cook over hot, not boiling, water, stirring frequently, until gelatin is completely dissolved. Stir in rum.

Refrigerate, stirring frequently, until mixture mounds slightly when dropped from spoon.

In large mixer bowl beat egg whites with cream of tartar until soft peaks form. Gradually add remaining 1/4 cup sugar and beat until stiff. Gently fold egg whites into rum custard. Spoon chocolate custard evenly into large wine goblets or stemmed glasses, then top with rum custard.

Garnish with chocolate curls.

Bread Pudding

6 slices of **Bread**, generously buttered
1 cup packed **Dark Brown Sugar**
1 tsp. **Cinnamon**
1/2 tsp. **Allspice**
2 **Eggs**
1/4 tsp. **Salt**
2 cups **Milk**
1/2 cup **Water**

Preheat oven to 325 degrees.

Dice buttered bread into 1-1/2 quart shallow pudding pan. Sprinkle with sugar and spices. Beat eggs with salt. Beat in milk and water. Pour over bread. Bake in preheated oven for about 30 minutes or until set.

Serves 6.

Bread Pudding—Chocolate

2 cups cubed **French Bread**
2 cups **Milk**
1 cup **Sugar**
1/2 cup **Unsweetened Cocoa**
1/2 tsp. **Cinnamon**
2 **Eggs**, beaten
1/2 cup **Raisins**
1/4 cup chopped **Pecans**
1 tbsp. melted **Butter**
2 tsp. **Vanilla**
Whipped Cream or **Ice Cream**, as desired

Preheat oven to 375 degrees.

Place bread cubes in a large bowl; add milk and let stand at least 10 minutes. Stir together sugar, cocoa and cinnamon. Combine eggs, raisins, pecans, butter and vanilla. Stir both mixtures into the bread and milk. Blend well and pour into an ungreased 10 x 6 x 2 inch baking dish (spray with Pam if desired).

Bake in preheated oven for 40 to 45 minutes or until knife inserted near center comes out clean.

Serve with whipped cream or ice cream. Serves 6 to 8.

Bread Pudding—Perfect

10 slices **Sweet French Bread**, crusts removed
5 tbsp. **Butter** (room temperature)
5 **Eggs**
4 **Egg Yolks**
1 cup **Sugar**
1/8 tsp. **Salt**
4 cups **Milk**
1 cup **Heavy Cream**
1 tbsp. **Vanilla**

Preheat oven to 375 degrees.

Butter one side of each slice of bread. Line a 3-quart glass-baking bowl with the bread, buttered side up. Set aside. Beat the eggs and yolks until blended. Strain them into a second large bowl. Add the sugar and salt to the egg mixture and stir to blend. Combine milk and cream and scald in a saucepan. Gradually add the hot milk mixture to the egg mixture, stirring constantly. Add the vanilla. Pour the custard into the bread lined baking dish. Put the bowl into a large, shallow roasting pan filled with enough boiling water to come up the sides of the bowl about 1-1/2 inches.

Bake the pudding in preheated oven about 45 minutes, 50 minutes at most. The center should be a little quivering.

Serve warm or cold with **Raspberry Sauce**. Serves 8-10.

Raspberry Sauce:

1 package (12 oz.) **Frozen Raspberries**, thawed and heated to just about boiling.

Thicken with **Cornstarch** and add some **Lemon Juice** to taste. Serve over bread. pudding.

Caramel Pudding

1 lb. **Sugar**
1/2 quart **Water**
12 **Eggs** (divided into 12 yolks and 6 whites)
1/4 cup **Sugar**
1 quart **Light Cream**
2 tsp. **Vanilla**

Preheat oven to 350 degrees.

Use iron skillet to prepare caramel. Boil sugar and water until it gets dry and melts again. Remove from heat when sugar starts getting light brown. Stir until desired color is reached—a deep golden brown. Pour evenly into lightly heated deep rectangular form covering bottom and all sides. Put aside to harden.

Beat 12 egg yolks and 6 egg whites with sugar. Boil cream with vanilla and pour into egg mixture while stirring. Let cool and pour into form with caramel.

Put form into pan half filled with hot water and bake in preheated oven for 1 1/2 hours. The water should boil slowly or pudding will curdle; as you check, oven termperature may be lowered. Turn carefully into serving platter.

Best made a day ahead. Serves 9 to 10.

Carmel Bread Pudding

1 cup **Brown Sugar**
4 slices **White Bread**, buttered
2 **Eggs**
3 cups **Milk**
Salt
Nutmeg

Preheat oven to 300 degrees.

Put brown sugar on bottom of 2-quart casserole dish. Butter 4 slices of white bread and break into small pieces, place on top of sugar. Beat eggs, add milk to eggs and pour over bread. DO NOT STIR. Sprinkle top with salt and nutmeg. Bake in preheated oven until a knife comes out clean—about 1 hour.

Chocolate Chip Filling

1 cup **Semi-Sweet Chocolate Chips**
1/2 cup **Butter**, room temperature
2/3 cup **Powdered Sugar**
2 **Egg Yolks**
1 tsp. **Vanilla**
2 **Egg Whites**

Melt chocolate chips and set aside. In a medium bowl, cream butter and powdered sugar until light and fluffy. Add egg yolks one at a time, beating well after each addition. Gradually beat in melted chips and vanilla. In a small bowl, beat egg whites until stiff, but not dry; fold into chocolate mixture. Use as a filling for cakes, cream puffs or éclairs.

Makes about 2 cups.

Lemon Jell-O® Dessert

2 small packages (3 oz. each) **Lemon Jell-O®**
2 cups **Boiling Water**
1 1/2 cups diced **Marshmallows**
1 large package (8 oz.) **Cream Cheese**
2 **Carrots**, grated
1 can (8 oz.) **Crushed Pineapple**
1 1/2 cups chopped **Walnuts**
1 pint **Whipping Cream**, whipped

Dissolve the packages of lemon Jell-O® into the boiling water; add the diced marshmallows and cream cheese. Stir until everything is dissolved. Add the carrots and the pineapple, juice and all. Add half of the whipped cream and half of the walnuts. Mix well. Pour mixture into a 13 x 9 x 2 inch pan; chill until firm.

Frost with the remaining whipped cream and sprinkle the remaining walnuts on top.

English Christmas Pudding

"In 1849, at the age of seven, my great, great grandmother, Margaret Capstick Leake, came to America from Yorkshire, England. This recipe was brought along on that voyage by her mother, also named Margaret."

Linda L. Leake, Palmyra

1 lb. **Ground Beef Suet**
1 lb. **White Bread,** crust removed and cubed
1 lb. **Brown Sugar**
1 lb. **White Flour**
1 lb. **Dark Raisins**
1 lb. **Currants**
4 **Eggs**
1 pint **Sweet Milk**
1 tsp. **Cinnamon**
1 tsp. **Cloves**
1 tsp. **Nutmeg**
Dash of **Salt**

Mix all ingredients together in a large bowl. Divide the dough into four (or two) portions, placing each portion in the center of a clean dish towel (not terry cloth) which has been sprinkled with flour. Tie each "bag" with cloth string (do not tie so tightly that there is no room for expansion, or so loosely that the pudding spills out). In a large kettle, steam the pudding bags for 2 1/2 hours (4 hours for two bags) on a rack in 1-2 inches of water. Bring the water to a rolling boil, and then reduce heat to maintain a gentle boil. Cover the kettle tightly with lid during the steaming; 30 to 60 minutes depending on size of bags. Pudding may also be frozen. Thaw before reheating.

Hard Sauce

1 cup **Water**
1/2 cup **Sugar**
2 tbsp. **Cornstarch**
1/4 cup **Butter**
1/4 cup **Lemon Juice**
2 tsp. grated **Lemon Rind**
Dash **Salt**
2 tbsp. **Brandy**

Place water in a saucepan; add sugar and cornstarch. Stir and bring to a boil. Reduce heat and stir until sauce is clear and thickened (about 5 minutes). Stir butter, lemon juice, rind and salt. Stir in brandy just before serving. Spoon hot sauce over hot pudding.

Römmegröt

(A Norwegian Cream Pudding)

"This recipe was brought from the 'old country' (as my mother would say) and was a basic dish served in Norwegian homes."

Edna M. Bjorgo—Gilmanton

1 quart **Sweet Cream**
1 cup **Flour**
2 1/2 cups **Scalded Milk**
1/2 tsp. **Salt**
3-4 tbsp. **Sugar**
Cinnamon

In a saucepan, bring cream to a boil, and stir constantly for about 5 minutes. Sift flour into mixture slowly, continuing to stir. Remove butterfat from top when it rises and reserve. Add scalded milk and beat well until mixture is velvety. Let simmer. Add salt and sugar. Remove from saucepan and put in a large bowl. Put reserved butterfat on top and sprinkle with sugar and cinnamon. Serve warm.

Date Pudding

"This is an old recipe that came from my dad's mother, and possibly from her mother."

Verna M. Prater—Belleville

1/2 stick **Butter**
1 cup packed **Light Brown Sugar**
2 cups **Boiling Water**
1/2 cup **Sugar**
1 cup **Flour**
2 tsp. **Baking Soda**
2/3 cup **Milk**
1 tsp. **Vanilla**
1 cup chopped **Dates**
1/2 cup chopped **Pecans**
Whipped Cream

Preheat oven to 375 degrees.

In the bottom of a 9x13 baking dish, place butter and brown sugar. Add boiling water and stir to dissolve sugar and melt butter. In a large bowl, mix together the remaining seven ingredients. Drop mixture by spoonfuls to layer evenly over sugar mixture in baking dish. Do not stir. Bake in preheated oven for 20-30 minutes. Serve warm or cold with whipped cream.

Mama Esther's Baked Custard

"A family favorite. My grandmother was Swedish and she loved to cook. I also serve this recipe for breakfast."

Bonnie McVoy-Verwys—Bonnie's Parsonage 1908 Bed & Breakfast—Holland

3 **Eggs**, beaten
1/2 cup **Sugar**
3 cups **Milk** (2% can be used)
Gound **Nutmeg**

Preheat oven to 300 degrees.

Combine eggs, sugar and milk. Pour into 6 ramekins and sprinkle nutmeg over tops. Set dishes in pan of water to ensure custard bakes evenly. Bake in preheated oven for 1 1/4 hours or until sharp knife inserted in custard comes out clean. Cool and refrigerate. Custard is good plain and/or served topped with fresh strawberries, along with traditional Dutch pigs-in-the-blanket, muffins, juice and a gourmet blend coffee. Serves 6.

Pecan Bread Pudding

1 cup **Sugar**
2 cups **Water**
1/2 cup **Molasses**
1 tsp. **Cinnamon**
1/4 tsp. **Cloves**
6 slices toasted **Bread**
1 1/2 cups grated **Longhorn Cheese**
1 cup **Raisins**
2 cups chopped **Pecans**

Preheat oven to 350 degrees.

Combine sugar, water, molasses, cinnamon and cloves. Boil until sugar is dissolved. In a buttered casserole, layer bread, cheese, raisins and pecans. Pour hot syrup over ingredients. Bake in preheated oven for 20-30 minutes, until syrup is absorbed.

Apple Pudding

"My grandmother often made this pudding and passed the recipe on to my mother. Our family has enjoyed it for years."

Patricia Bailey—Libby

1/4 cup **Butter**
1 cup **Sugar**
1 **Egg**
1 1/2 cups grated **Apple**
1 cup **Flour**
1 tsp. **Baking Soda**
1/2 tsp. **Cinnamon**
1/2 tsp. **Nutmeg**
1/4 tsp. **Salt**
1/4 cup fresh **Cranberries**
1/4 cup chopped **Pecans**
1/4 cup **Raisins**

Preheat oven to 350 degrees.

In a bowl, cream butter, sugar and eggs together until fluffy. Stir in apples. In another bowl, sift together dry ingredients and then add to creamed mixture. Fold in cranberries, nuts and raisins. Spread pudding in a greased 13 × 9 baking pan. Bake in preheated oven for 45 minutes. Serve with vanilla yogurt or cream.

Grandmas come in all shapes and sizes…all styles and personalities…and live in all parts of the world. But there seems to be universal affection for grandmas that transcends fashion, geography, and politics. I think six-year-old Carrie said it best. "I love my gramma 'cause she loves *me*…and she always smells like cookies!"

Index

The Artist

Debbie Bell Jarratt, born in Philadelphia, Pennsylvania, began her professional career in art when she joined the design staff at Hallmark Cards in Kansas City, Missouri. She has designed for such companies as Enesco, The Franklin Mint, Goebel, Thomas Nelson Publishers, C.R. Gibson and many more.

Debbie's art appears on millions of products in the form of greeting cards, a variety of collectibles and books.

She now lives in North Carolina with her family. You can see more of Debbie's work on her website, www.debbiebelljarrattgallery.com

The Author

Michael Liddy was destined for cooking when at age eight, his grandmother caught him frying baloney in a pan. She affectionately called him "Baloney Bubble" and from then on, he hasn't stopped cooking! From his first job at a modest butcher shop in New Jersey to family restaurants, hospitals, and the famous Arizona Biltmore Hotel, Michael has honed his cooking skills and earned the title "chief cook and bottle washer." Now Michael works for himself in the catering business, which allows him time to test recipes for his cookbooks!

Michael loves cooking and sharing his life with his wife, Dawn, four children, Elizabeth, Alyssa, Dylon, Taylor and new granddaughter, McKenzy. Besides his passion for cooking, Liddy is an excellent musician and tours with "oldies" music artists throughout the country.

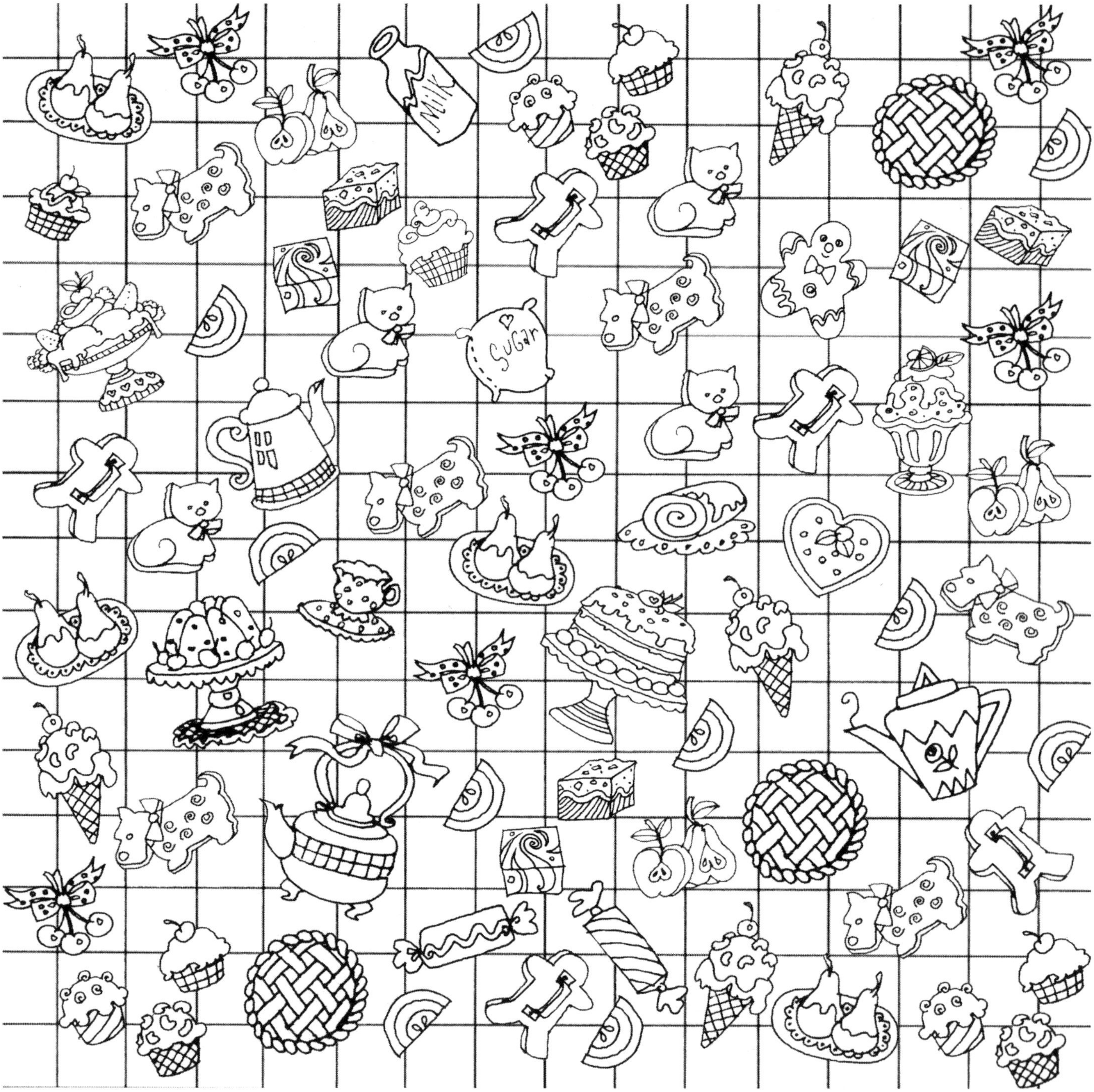
MILK
SUGAR